Mornings on Fair Oaks Bridge

Watching Wildlife at the Lower American River

Writing & photography by Janice Kelley

Mornings on Fair Oaks Bridge

Mornings on Fair Oaks Bridge/ Janice Kelley -- 1st ed.
ISBN 978-0-9715467-2-1

This book is dedicated to all wildlife living along the American River Parkway. May they always be safe from harm and live in peace through all seasons of the year. Special thanks to all individuals, organizations and groups who protect this vital waterway.

Mornings on Fair Oaks Bridge

"These beautiful days must enrich all my life.
They do not exist as mere pictures. . . but they saturate themselves
into every part of the body and live always.

John Muir

CONTENTS

2018

INTRODUCTION

——

I look forward to every morning on Fair Oaks Bridge when I discover and celebrate gifts of the outdoor world.

MORNINGS ARE A PEACEFUL AND MAGICAL TIME on the American River at Fair Oaks Bridge. The chill of the morning creates dewdrops on the bridge and deck. Winter fog blankets the landscape and rolls slowly downriver floating above the surface of the water. Stunning sunrises paint clouds in deep pinks and orange long before the glowing sun is visible over distant trees. Resident waterfowl engage in early morning rituals, dunking, patrolling, snapping at bugs and cleaning their feathers to prepare for the new day. A dozen pigeons fly over three times before landing on the bridge frame or walking the deck searching for food. Birds heard in the distance, sing a variety of soft melodies. Fall fishermen bear cold temperatures and wind waiting for the perfect moment when they catch a salmon to bring home. Spiders spin intricate webs on the side rails of Fair Oaks Bridge to snare small insects.

I woke one Sunday morning in September 2016 and impulsively decided to visit the Fair Oaks Bridge at 6:30 am to see what happens there at daybreak. I have visited the bridge and rode my bicycle along the river for years. This time I focused my attention on what happens during early mornings. I visited every morning for a week at the same time to observe what may change from day to day. I discovered each day presented a new series of experiences. This was the beginning of my *Morning on Fair Oaks Bridge* blogs. I came to observe, write, photograph and capture in video the scenic beauty, and the essence of daily rituals, antics, and changing dynamics of the relationships among wildlife living at the American River alongside Fair Oaks Bridge.

After my first week, visiting Fair Oaks Bridge a few mornings a week became my wake up ritual and created a great meditative foundation for my day. I kept going through the fall, a few times during our stormy, wet winter to witness the flooding, resumed frequent visits in spring and our rare solar eclipse, and through the summer. I kept going through my second year and continue to visit, write and photograph. Most mornings at Fair Oaks Bridge begin in Fair Oaks Village, listening to chickens greet me with their good morning songs before walking to the bridge.

Mornings on Fair Oaks Bridge

My backpack, journal and camera are constant companions. Sometimes I don't have words to express the joy and delight of these experiences. The beauty of the quiet mornings is a far deeper experience than the act of writing words on a page or taking photos can express. I sit and listen. I watch and wonder. I have learned to appreciate that wildlife undisturbed live by their own rhythms as we watch in silence.

After a year of observations and learning morning wildlife wake up patterns, I decided to create a book to share a full year of seasonal changes, wildlife dynamics and my experiences on the American River. This collection includes selected blog posts that extend from September 2016 through February 2018.

Many narratives pose questions, such as "why?" and "where are?" Some reflect on larger concerns about the need to preserve critical habitat. Other entries highlight the simple pleasure of being in the right place at the right time. These observations are opportunities for readers and visitors to experience the "magic of mornings on Fair Oaks Bridge," through more than a year of sunrises, fog, rain and chill.

Discover morning wildlife wake up patterns and curious interactions between the area's abundant wildlife: chicken symphonies heard across Fair Oaks Village, pigeon dances over the bridge, bird song greetings, and the flights of Canada Geese, ducks, seagulls, Egrets, Great Blue Heron and Cormorants. Meet turtles, beaver and river otter along the way.

Mornings on Fair Oaks Bridge is my gift to readers, visitors and viewers who find joy and peace by observing and experiencing the wonders and curiosities of the outdoor world. I invite you to find your own special place of peace to pause, reflect, discover and learn.

Janice Kelley, October 2018

BACKGROUND

———

Introductions to Fair Oaks Village, Fair Oaks Bridge, Fair Oaks Bluff and the American River Parkway on the following pages are part of much larger community stories tied to the suburban development of Sacramento and the need to preserve its natural resources. These introductions provide background on settings described in the book.

Learn more about these places from the Fair Oaks Historical Society, Fair Oaks Village Enhancement Committee, American River Parkway Foundation, Save the American River Association, American River Natural History Association and Sacramento County Regional Parks. These are some of the many local and statewide agencies that work collaboratively to help preserve and protect local resources, and provide information and educational programs.

Read additional *Mornings on Fair Oaks Bridge* blogs and find information about workshops and other activities, podcasts of selected blogs and photo gallery at https://naturelegacies.com.

I hope you enjoy these early morning walks. *Thank you for being here!*

FAIR OAKS VILLAGE

———

Agricultural roots, parks, dining, entertainment, and chickens to add their own kind of music

Nisenan Indians were the first residents of what is now Fair Oaks. After the Nisenan left, the area became part of the 1844 Mexican Land Grant of Rancho San Juan. Fair Oaks was officially established in 1895 as one of several agricultural colonies settled in the Sacramento area. Perspective residents often arrived by train from the Midwest to begin farming or grow vineyards in the area's fertile soil with the blessing of fair weather. Fair Oaks is an unincorporated community of Sacramento County.

Fair Oaks Village has always been the community's center of activity. Two Village parks are the setting for summer concerts, an amphitheater, and three annual festivals. May is *Fair Oaks Fiesta* with a classic car show. The *Chicken Festival* happens in September. *Christmas in the Village* is the first weekend in December. The Community Center/Clubhouse hosts recreational activities, classes and community group meetings. The Fair Oaks Coffee House and Deli, presents live entertainment and serves as a daytime gathering place for great food and conversation. Fair Oaks Brew Pub enjoys daytime regulars and hosts the Village nightlife. These sites are the heartbeat of the Village. Sunflower Natural Foods Drive-in is another favorite for residents and out of area visitors. Village streets, lined with historic buildings from the earliest days of Fair Oaks, feature assorted gift shops, a BBQ store, flower shop and other independent businesses. Fair Oaks History Center offers self-guided walking tours.

Fair Oaks Chickens

Many residents and visitors believe the active and abundant Fair Oaks Village chickens add character and charm to this hidden gem. Their squabbles, persistent calls to each other, and continuous patrols of Village streets and parks provide a different kind of entertainment. Parks and neighboring streets are the daily setting for their rousing morning symphony. They are regular members of the community, often insisting on being involved in special events and leading parades. Residents and visitors take their pictures, give them food, and watch their antics. Cars driving through the Village stop and wait for chickens to meander across streets. When mama chicken brings her babies across a street, rooster dad stands in the center giving all drivers an evil eye until the family is safely across. Drivers wait, honk their

horns and wait some more. Groups of two, three or four chickens often gather for conferences in parking lots. These chickens tend to hang out in pairs or in a group – unless one has been chased away after a noisy squabble. During the heat of summer, they rest alongside a tree in the park. The hen in the center was eager to get my attention by sitting next to my laptop. The biggest roosters have the longest and deepest calls. The smallest chickens sound more like coughing with a scratchy throat. Even thin and scrawny, the smallest chickens behave as if they were the big roosters.

FAIR OAKS BRIDGE

———

A Historic and Treasured Icon

FAIR OAKS BRIDGE is a link to the community's agricultural past and connecting point from Fair Oaks Village for walkers, runners and cyclists to reach the American River Parkway and the Jedediah Smith Memorial Bicycle Trail. This nearly 500–foot span across the river is an ideal place to watch the sunrise, sunsets, and moonrises with unobstructed views. Wildlife and birds engage in their daily rituals on or near the bridge most of the year. As a result of its historical significance, Fair Oaks Bridge was placed on the National Register of Historic Places in September 2006.

The original bridge was completed in 1901. The Sacramento-Placerville Railroad extended a line to the Fair Oaks Bridge to give new resident farmers a way to ship their farm produce. The railway station also gave residents easy access to the city of Sacramento. Severe flooding of 1907 caused the bridge to collapse and was not rebuilt. A second, temporary bridge took its place until a new, permanent bridge could be completed. The temporary bridge lasted until another flood and collapsed in 1909.

Fair Oaks Bridge as it stands now is a metal Truss bridge – meaning that the connecting parts of the bridge are triangles and use concrete piers as supports. It officially opened for auto traffic in 1909. Fair Oaks Bridge was once the main vehicle crossing for the American River before constructing three other area bridges. It closed to vehicle traffic in 1967. The County of Sacramento now owns the bridge. The railroad station, no longer in use, was removed when the American River Parkway was built.

Source: Fair Oaks Historical Society

Fog moves on surface of American River. View of Fair Oaks Bridge from boat launch ramp (facing northwest)

FAIR OAKS BLUFF

———

Grass roots efforts preserved visitor access to impressive panoramic views

Sacramento County was once part of an extensive inland sea on the western edge of the North American Continental Plate. Geologic forces created the mountain ranges as the Continental Plate was pushed under the Oceanic Plate. The mountains cut off the sea, causing marine life to die and eventually become fossils. Looking at the face of Fair Oaks Bluff, materials near the water line were deposited about 700,000 years ago. Other lines in the Bluff represent glacial activity ranging from 300,000 to 10,000 years ago. Water rushing down the American River corridor from the Sierra Nevada into the Sacramento Valley over time cut away the hillside, exposing striations in the rock, and eventually formed the Fair Oaks Bluff we see today.

The area is now protected as part of the Sacramento County Regional Park System thanks to *Citizens to Save Fair Oaks Bluff.* This grass roots organization launched a major fund raising campaign in 2000 to purchase 4.5 acres at the edge of the Bluff. Their goal was to create public access to open space at the top of the 140-feet cliff. Standing at the top of the cliff, visitors face the American River Parkway and enjoy spectacular, unobstructed views of the Sierra Nevada to the east. On a clear day, views can extend to Mt. Diablo located in the San Francisco Bay Area on the western horizon.

During a five-year effort, the community raised $1.3 million from 1,500 donors, ranging from $5 to $50,000. Sacramento County, the Raley Foundation, Fair Oaks Recreation and Park District, and the Sacramento County Board of Supervisors provided major support to complete this community preservation project.

Source: Excerpted from interpretive panels developed by Sacramento County Regional Parks and the County of Sacramento. Panels are located on Bridge Street near the entrance to Fair Oaks Bridge at the base of the trail leading to the Bluff.

Donor names etched on brick create an entry plaza for path to Fair Oaks Bluff.

AMERICAN RIVER PARKWAY

—

Preserving Open Space and riparian habitat

The American River Parkway is a 23-mile greenbelt that encases the Lower American River and winds often unseen through Sacramento's suburban communities where more than one and half million people live. The Parkway begins Northeast of Sacramento at the Folsom Dam and extends southwest to the confluence of the American and Sacramento Rivers near the city's historic waterfront. Referred to as the *Jewel of Sacramento*, the Parkway features shimming waters, dense oak woodlands, wide, open spaces and steep bluffs. Hikers, cyclists, bird watchers and equestrians enjoy an expansive network of trails with panoramic views of the river, in addition to wildlife feeding and nesting areas. The Parkway also provides easy access for fishing, rafting and kayaking.

*From the birth of the idea to create a parkway, community residents and advocates, governmental and nonprofit agencies have worked collaboratively over many years to acquire property, secure funding, preserve habitat, wildlife, recreation opportunities, and assure its safety and upkeep. ***

The initial concept for a parkway plan surfaced in the late 1940s with support from the Sacramento Chamber of Commerce, the city and county. Sacramento County began land acquisitions along the American River between 1950 and 1980. In 1959, Sacramento County established a Department of Parks and Recreation. William Pond, the first Development Director moved the parkway idea forward, finding strong support for a trail and paved path among numerous user groups. Save the River Association (SARA) was born in 1961 to rally community support for preserving river and adjacent habitat and prohibit encroaching development plans. Pond and other key community leaders, including local naturalist Effie Yeaw, Jim Jones and James C. Mullaney led grass roots efforts. Based on community support, the Sacramento County Board of Supervisors adopted the first Parkway Plan. The Parkway Plan has been updated numerous times over the years. The most recent update was in 2008.

The American River Natural History Association (ARNHA) was founded in 1981 to support educational and interpretive activities in the American River Parkway. The American River Parkway Foundation supports the preservation and enjoyment of the Parkway by fostering environmental education, stewardship and volunteer opportunities.

*Source: unknown

SEPTEMBER 2016

FIRST MORNINGS

———

Roosters patrol Fair Oaks Village greeting each day with their wake up songs. I think of this as a chicken symphony because one calls and the others respond in sequence. Each morning brings a new experience at Fair Oaks Bridge.

WATCHING WILDLIFE WAKE UP

Sunday, September 18, 2016, 6:35 am

WHEN I FIRST ARRIVE AT FAIR OAKS BRIDGE, the sun has yet to rise over distant trees on the opposite riverbank. I focus my attention on the landscape and notice so many different habitats for wildlife. The roosters are the most obvious. In previous visits, I have seen Great Blue Herons on the river, Egrets, Canada Geese and many species of ducks. I saw an owl only once and occasionally river otters. Trees, fallen logs, shrubs, and the island farther upstream are excellent hiding places. The river itself creates homes too. The bridge is home to bats hidden underneath in specially formed concrete grooves.

Two walkers approach and tell me a beaver family lives between Sunrise Blvd. and Jim's pedestrian bridge farther west down the river. To catch a glimpse of them, I need to be at the river by 6:30 when they search for food.

Six boats of fisherman are lined up on the river and waiting patiently with their fishing lines cast in the green water. I suppose there must be fish to catch. I don't see any jumping. Spiders spin webs all over the bridge snaring a feast of flies. Every beam is strung with spider webs. *Hmmm. Where are the spiders?* I see two large webs as the final resting place for close to 50 flies hanging loose in the air like a tiny net blowing in the wind. I get tangled in one of their hanging threads because I was too close walking past them.

At this early hour, 30 minutes after dawn, people are walking their dogs, and cyclists in riding gear with backpacks speed across the bridge.

Roosters patrol Fair Oaks Village greeting each day with their wake up calls. One chicken calls and another one responds. These messages are heard throughout the village, up in the trees, down the neighborhood streets and on the bike trail, *Hey, I am awake. Pay attention!* I have seen and heard them everywhere – crowing even when no one is in sight.

Canada Geese fly overhead. Birds chatter. One tiny bird sits on top of the bridge and calls out, "*Chi Choo...Chi Choo.*" I watch its whole small body and tail shake with every call. It jumps from beam to beam trying its best to catch someone's attention.

CYCLISTS, WALKERS AND WILDLIFE MEET

MONDAY, SEPTEMBER 19, 2016, 7 AM

BRIGHT LIGHT REFLECTS ON THE WATER. A cool breeze blows across my face. Today, unlike yesterday, a loud hum echoes from the Sunrise Blvd. Bridge crossing as early risers drive to and from Highway 50. Roosters have already finished their morning wake up calls. A few stragglers are still crowing. Two men float in their boats with fishing lines cast. More cyclists pass by this morning than the same time yesterday. Walkers are out with their dogs. The moment I walk onto the bridge an Egret flies in on the west side and quickly hides in shrubs at the riverbank. Ducks swim in pairs, searching for breakfast nibbles on insects.

As the sun rises, the water's reflection is so bright I squint looking east toward the boat launch ramp. I hear the distinctive calls of many birds. I see none. The full moon sits in the western sky.

Bicycles and heavy footsteps vibrate the bridge deck. Walkers, runners, and dog walkers say *Good morning* as they pass. Some give a nod and keep their focus on walking straight ahead. I enjoy the sweet smell of morning. In a few weeks, the gentle breeze will carry the odor of decaying salmon that have completed their journey home to spawn.

FAIR OAKS BLUFF REFLECTIONS

TUESDAY, SEPTEMBER 20, 2016, 7 AM

ROOSTERS CALL "GOOD MORNING" while hidden for the night in trees and shrubs. Some early risers wander about in the street.

A lone kayaker approaches the boat ramp after an early morning row. Two men in a boat cast fishing rods into the water. I see the same women jogging today and wonder how many people come here regularly?

Birds sit on the bridge frame surveying the landscape. Ducks come out searching for breakfast. Dabbling ducks turn tail side up to take a look under water. Just like a buoy, they bob back up and their tail flops down. Dive. Heads up, Bubbles circle their heads and down they go again.

The sun rises over the trees, casting light on the Fair Oaks Bluff on the north side of the American River. Oak trees cling to the bluff. Parts of their root systems are exposed and hang loosely over the cliff edge. An Egret flies across the river low and slow and dives under a bush. Water is shallow. The deep emerald green water is shallow and completely opaque. As the water ripples, the sun reflects fuzzy shadows of the Bluff in the river.

WATERFOWL WALK AND SKI

———

WEDNESDAY, SEPTEMBER 21, 2016, 7 AM

CLOUDS COVER THE SKY. RAINDROPS FALL ON MY WINDSHIELD. In the 10 minutes it takes to walk to the river, the sky has already brightened. Raindrops that fall on Fair Oaks Bridge evaporate quickly. I feel a cool breeze blow against my face. This is the first moisture of late summer and in a few minutes the drizzle has passed.

Roosters wake up the neighborhood with their calls – one crowing and another responds. Far fewer roosters are awake today. Maybe the chill has kept them hiding in trees.

I know the morning sun has risen over the horizon. Yet I cannot see it hidden behind dense cloud cover.

A Great Blue Heron walks gingerly along the riverbank, placing each step with care and inspecting every inch for a bit of breakfast. A flock of a dozen Canada Geese fly in over the bridge. They turn sharply to the north and fly toward Fair Oaks Village. Now two Herons are visiting the river on this morning of stillness.

Fishermen in three boats sit and wait for salmon to bite. The water is too cloudy to see if any are swimming nearby. The only cyclist I see speeds by wearing a helmet light. A man and woman walk toward the Village carrying a large sleeping bag. Reading their expressions, they enjoyed spending an evening outdoors and were on their way home.

The moon, visible in the western sky, slowly fades away. A pinkish glow behind the clouds has vanished. The sun is still hidden. As clouds part, the blue sky displays a range of hues from dark bluish gray to gray to bright white. Drops fall again on the bridge, leaving a collage of dots. A flock of about 50 pigeons dance in the air above my head. I wonder what morning symphony they are listening to? Other birds nearby tweet and respond to their friends across the water. Roosters hide in trees on the riverbank sounding their morning calls. The air does not have the smell of rain, even as the drops fall. I feel the heavy heat of the day to come, even at 7:25 am. Have yet to see any one walking on the Fair Oaks Bluff. With the air warming, pigeons return to their stations on the bridge. The beaver family remains elusive, apparently preferring the privacy beyond the Sunrise bridge crossing. Still too early to see salmon begin their ritual leaps. While I sit and watch wildlife wake up on the bridge, the cyclists rumble by on their way across. Some ride for pleasure. Others race by, clad in full color riding attire with their backpacks.

I enjoy watching ducks and geese fly in for landing in the water. They drop down to within a foot of the water, then stretch out their legs in front of them, ski on their webbed feet as brakes until they land into the water, sit down and fold their wings. I wonder if I will ever see a mother duck give her ducklings flying lessons? How do ducks learn to fly?

WAITING FOR SALMON

———

THURSDAY, SEPTEMBER 22, 2016, 7:15 AM

BY THE TIME I ARRIVE AT FAIR OAKS BRIDGE, the sun has already risen high above the trees, glowing yellow and hot in a cloudless sky. The bridge is filled with sunlight. Morning walkers pass by. We exchange good mornings and smiles. Garage doors lift and shut as residents of the Village drive on to the street and away to begin their workday. A young boy in a boat struggles with his fishing pole. The boy gives up, tosses the pole and begins to explore the boat, walking back and forth, checking its bottom for something interesting to examine.

Five boats are filled with fisherman who cast their lines into the cloudy green water. The boats sit at some distance apart on the east side of the bridge. Thousands of salmon will be arriving soon, jumping randomly out the water. They have not yet arrived from their long journey from the Pacific, through the Delta sloughs, up the Sacramento River and into the American River. Many salmon will end their journey near the Fair Oaks Bridge. Others will swim upriver another two miles to the weir (type of fence) and intuitively swim up the fish ladder at the Nimbus Fish Hatchery to spawn.

Salmon are truly amazing, navigating the entire journey using their sense of smell and genetic code to direct them back to their home river.

This tiny bird sits in its usual place on the upper frame of the bridge calling *Ti Too...Ti Too.* I watch its whole body shake and tail flutter as speaking its good morning call. I wonder if it is saying good morning or scolding me for invading its privacy.

I wonder why birds return to the same spot on the bridge frame? Is this like our returning home to sit in the same comfortable chair? Do roosters and chickens fly to the same tree branch to hide and sleep for the night? I wonder what they say to each other? Are they speaking to the people they meet on the bicycle trail?

Spider webs, spiders and the insects snared in webs hang on side rails and the truss frame.

COMING OF FALL

———

Friday, September 23, 2016, 7 am, 53 degrees

I FINALLY ACKNOWLEDGE THE PASSING OF LONG, WARM SUMMER DAYS when the cool mornings of October arrive. Days when sunlight and bike rides along the American River last until 9 pm are passed. Dew covers my car windshield in the morning now. The air is chilled at 645 am. My first Sunday morning on Fair Oaks Bridge, I wore shorts and a t-shirt, and warmed quickly by the sun. Today, I wear my denim jacket and slip on a pair of jeans. Yesterday's morning temperature was 55. Today it is 53. As days grow shorter, and fall blends into winter, morning temperatures will drop further to 45 and then 35 and sometimes the high 20s.

Determined fishermen sit in their boats waiting. Others walk into the American River or fish from an island. They come before dawn to catch the salmon. I notice the moon in the sky. During my first Sunday, the moon was full. Today, hardly a week later, the moon is now half visible.

Bicyclists carrying backpacks roar across the bridge this morning before sunrise. The pigeons have returned, taking their places on the bridge. Even when pigeons are gone, anyone can tell where they sit. The edges of the bridge on each side are spotted with white droppings. Today they arrive without their ritual dance and quickly position themselves for a morning nap.

The colors of sunrise change from pale pink to deep orange. Reflections on either side of the river below are still fuzzy from the constant ripples of water. Other parts of the river shine like mirrors.

I walk to the boat launch ramp to feed ducks and geese. Once the feeding starts, other ducks swim over as fast as they can go. Some too impatient to swim, rise out of the water and flap their wings for 10 yards to speed their arrival. I throw to my left to attract attention, then to my right. I throw food to a quiet dozen ducks. Three fly in and more swim over. The crowd gets noisy. Some are fighting over the food, biting and squawking. Others are chased away. The noise gets even louder. *Quack! Quack! Quack!* Ducks dart from left to right, swimming in circles to capture the food.

Some open their beak and the food falls right in to mash and swallow. Within minutes 30 ducks circle and wait and quack and complain. Several walk up the boat launch ramp to get closer to the source. Canada Geese are usually late to arrive. They merge into the crowd to get something for themselves.

When the food is gone, the group realizes the excitement is over. As quickly as they arrived, ducks disburse and swim back to where they came from. The morning grooming ritual begins. Some enjoy a leisurely swim before settling down near the riverbank in the shade of overhanging trees. They are intent on watching fisherman waiting patiently to catch a fish.

OCTOBER 2016

———

I celebrate each time ducks and geese land in the water. They extend their thin legs at a slight angle. As soon as their feet splash into the water, they ski a few feet, fold their wings and sit down. Landings last only seconds.

DRESSING UP

SATURDAY, OCTOBER 1, 2016, 8:50 AM, 57 DEGREES

I ARRIVE AND CHECK FOR NEW SPIDER WEBS AND SPIDERS. Where are the spiders? So many webs line the bridge rails without any spiders. I keep looking. Maybe the temperatures are too cool? I have walked the bridge many times in summer, and seen a dozen spiders doing their daily work.

Cyclists in matching attire rumble past me. Always in a hurry, speeding by as fast as they can ride. The only words ever spoken are "on your left" or "bikes up." The bridge shakes when cyclists pass by. Even a heavy runner causes the bridge to vibrate. Pairs of walkers engaged in deep conversation pass by not even looking to either side of the bridge.

I see a man walking two small Scotty dogs. Both dogs wear scarves around their necks. I ask, *"Why are your dogs wearing scarves? Do scarves keep them warm?"* He says, *"No. They look cute in scarves. We like them dressed this way when they go out."*

The pigeons sit above me dropping obvious clues on the bridge where they spend most of their time. They speak loudly in a language of rhythmic "coos" that only pigeons can understand.

I bring food today and walk to the boat launch ramp to get closer to the ducks and geese. One duck and one Canada Goose notice me first. Within seconds, ducks fly in from the shady shoreline. Those that don't want to swim, fly in. I celebrate each time ducks and geese land in the river. They land with their thin legs extended and splash into the water. As soon as their feet touch the water, they fold their wings and sit down. Landings last only seconds.

I toss feed all around and behind me. Ducks walk up the boat ramp to get closer to the food. Geese stand beside me hoping for some favoritism by coming close. I make sure they all get an equal chance. Ducks bite and fight and swim away scolded. This is a common problem when three-dozen ducks show up for breakfast. Someone is always getting scolded and driven away from the crowd.

A rowboat comes up the ramp and the ducks scatter with a chorus of angry *"Quack, Quack"* and a frantic flutter of wings. Ducks move 50 yards to the east to a shady, protected spot. Getting on with their daily routine, ducks swim away in a straight line of three. As they swim away, I hear the third one in line complain with a series of unending *"Quack, Quack,"* while the other two ignore the chatter.

GREAT DAY FOR A LEISURELY SWIM OR DIP!

—

MONDAY, OCTOBER 3, 2016, 6 PM, 70 DEGREES

CLOUDS RESEMBLE STRIPS OF PALE BLUE AND WHITE COTTON CANDY. At 6 pm, no sun to be found. The air feels cool and I wear my zip up hooded sweatshirt. No birds out. A few ducks are out for a leisurely swim. I hear splashes in the water, look to the sound and see rings of concentric circles. Was it a salmon that jumped out and dove back in quickly? Since my last visit I see that rain has fallen on the bridge. The intricate networks of spider webs and flytraps are washed clean off the bridge upright and cross beams. Not a trace is left. The air is heavy with the scent of moist dirt, yet clean and refreshed by gentle rain.

Two boats and a kayak sit in the water. A few cyclists pass and walkers out for an evening stretch before sunset. I walk to the boat launch ramp and the ducks see me coming. A dozen ducks gather and walk up the ramp and wait. They look at me impatiently as if to say, *Where is the food?* Ducks go upside down for a dip! After a few minutes when they realize I have no food, they retreat back into the water. In minutes some have disappeared to hiding places on either side of the ramp.

The clouds spread apart and change color. A pale pink streak stretches wide across the eastern sky. Looking west, the sky is still blanketed with gray, puffy clouds. Today, the bridge is quiet. Walkers come to stand and watch the wildlife and changing colors of the sky.

What is the story behind this painted picture on the bridge?
Is this a soldier saluting?

Walking up the boat ramp I hear a wild chorus from ducks swimming toward me in the river. I am certain they are scolding me with their quacks, "*Be sure you bring food next time!*"

I wonder if ducks have nightly rituals? Human parents give baths and read bedtime stories. Children are tucked into soft beds and fall asleep. What can ducks do to prepare for nighttime? I can imagine what the chickens do because every morning they crow from trees, completely hidden from view until it is warm enough to fly down into the park and village streets.

Darkness will arrive within the hour. The pinks in the clouds have faded to gray. The moment the sun has set below the horizon, the sky already seems a shade darker. I love watching sunset at the bridge because reflected shadows change with the light. Reflections in the water are often mirror images of Fair Oaks Bluff. By nightfall, the shadows change. Edges of the trees and all plants on either side of the bridge are extra sharp and clear as the sun begins to set. I feel a chill in the air the moment the sun drops below the horizon. In another 30 minutes, it will be dark.

SALMON JUMP EVERY DAY BEFORE SUNRISE

———

FRIDAY, OCTOBER 7, 2016, 6:30 AM, 50 DEGREES

THE COLORS OF SUNRISE ARE SHADES OF PINKS AND ORANGES as the sun shines through scattered clouds. So far, roosters crowing to wake up the day are the only living creatures I see moving. No cars or people are outside yet. A few minutes later, several cyclists pass me wearing red blinking lights that shine through the darkness. Airplanes fly over and leave glowing white tails behind them.

My hands are chilled. These morning temperatures are a long way from 85-degrees only a few weeks ago. Pigeons fly in under the bridge from the west about 7 am. They appear to respond to an internal clock related to air temperature and moment of sunrise. They take their usual places on the bridge. This time they come quietly with no music or grand entrance. The tiny bird has flown to one of the tallest cross beams of the bridge. It calls, *Ti...Too. Ti...Too.*

Six boats line up on the water waiting for their opportunities to catch salmon. The first boats on the river sit in darkness with red lights blinking near the bridge. Salmon jump up and then quickly down. I wonder if fish are teasing the fishermen, *Come on and catch me! You better be quick!* I see the fish jumping again and again only 20 feet from one boat. No one cast a fishing line in that direction.

BUSY MORNING FOR SALMON FISHERMEN

———

WEDNESDAY, OCTOBER 12, 2016, 6:30 AM, 52 DEGREES

MORNING AIR IS FILLED WITH MOISTURE. Car windows are covered with dew. Roosters, still in hiding, begin their morning music and suddenly stop. The morning sky is scattered with clouds that cover the sun. A deep, dark orange slowly fades to gray. Under the bridge, the fishing boats are very busy. Salmon are jumping. I watch as three salmon bite on fishing lines. Fishermen sitting in their boats a few yards from the bridge catch the fish and scoop them into nets. This is so far, the busiest morning of the season.

More than 20 pigeons arrive about 7 am to fly their morning circle and quickly disappear. On this chilly morning, I watch them come and circle the bridge a half dozen times. They fly in, circle, and vanish into the distance; then repeat the flying pattern over and over again.

Photo at right shows a salmon caught in a net. A fisherman standing in rapids ready for a full day outside with his chair, water and cooler chest is pictured on following page.

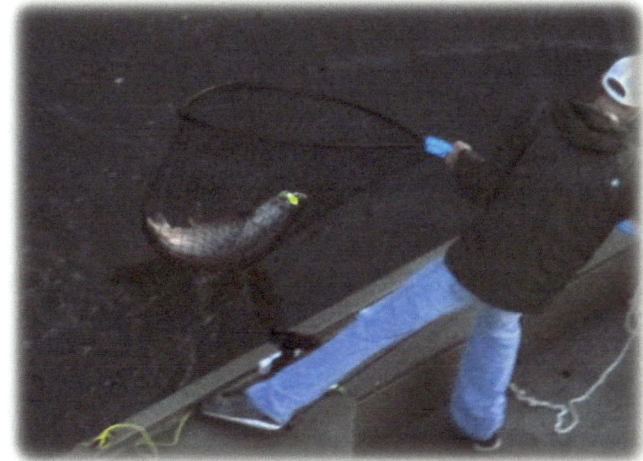

Mornings on Fair Oaks Bridge

WATCHING WILDLIFE

———

SATURDAY, OCTOBER 22, 2016, 5 PM

KAYAKS LAUNCH AND CHILDREN ENJOY FEEDING DUCKS ON THE BOAT RAMP. Other visitors stand on the bridge to watch the activity. Evening hours always inspire people to enjoy the river and watch wildlife, boats and the setting sun. Fishermen wait for a bite on their fishing lines.

Riding along the parkway this afternoon, I heard the distinctive sound of a woodpecker working in a nearby tree and stopped to watch. We may call it pecking. Officially, they *drum*. I watched the woodpecker at work near the top of the tree for several minutes until it decided to fly across the road to another tree.

I ride to another one of my favorite scenic spots and see a dozen turkey vultures sitting in the treetops. They sit in treetops on bare branches. I wonder if turkey vultures want a clear view of the landscape to scout for their next meal? Two walkers approach and they tell me about a dead baby deer that lay in their yard for only a day. The next day Turkey vultures ate everything, including the bones.

Fishermen's island paradise on American River – site becomes "Rocky Remnants" after flooding.

LIGHT RAIN REFRESHES THE MORNING

Tuesday, October 25, 2016, 11:15 am, 68 degrees

LIGHT RAIN STARTS AND STOPS. Still few people are outside. Warm rain. A quiet river. Sky is covered with dense clouds. Ducks search the river for food as wings flap. Faint quacks. Canada Geese change position and fly away. Boaters sit calmly in the water. The gentle, nourishing rain is a refreshing and welcome change.

Early morning boaters in their rain jackets have sped away, heading east. Birds patrol the sky. Turkey vultures wait patiently. They are ready to pounce on whatever has died. I find salmon heads cast off on to rocks. Soon hungry turkey vultures, seagulls, geese or other wildlife will consume these remains.

Thirty pigeons line the boat ramp. In an instant they rise in unison and fly to settle on the bridge truss frame. Two ducks hide at the riverbank and watch the rain.

As I see seagulls fly over the river, I think of the story of Jonathan Livingston Seagull soaring over the ocean. An Egret flies overhead, wings flapping ever so gently as it moves swiftly and silently, until out of sight. The river is so still not even an oak leaf is moving. The air is punctuated with scent of dead salmon masking the sweet smell of freshly fallen rain.

It is drizzling again and the ducks are taking shelter. Farther along the trail I find ducks dunking in a shallow pool. Shallow levels of the river provide more places for ducks and other shore birds to find food. I rarely

ride my bike in rain. Today I am richly rewarded. A coyote walks in front of me on the bike trail and veers off the trail to the right as soon as he sees me. He waits for me to come closer. As I approach, looks over his shoulder and then vanishes into the brush. Just up the road not a minute later, I hear a rustle in the bushes and see only the head and shoulders of a deer. It carries a full set of antlers, rushes through the brush and disappears.

A seagull reigns over the river on a small rock – just his size and completely surrounded by water – as if to stay, *I claim this space as mine and the salmon will come to me.* I watch, listen and hear the call of seagulls. I wonder how do they know their way here? Do they follow the salmon from the ocean? Do they search for landmarks?

Drizzle begins again. Runners and cyclists are still out. Birds chatter. *Kee kee ewe, kee, kee, ewe.*

So much to watch, so much to listen for and so much I want to capture to share, I need one part of me to watch and listen, one part of me to write, and another to take photos. I miss the salmon jumping while I am watching the ducks squabble and dunk. I miss seeing the Egret that flies in, as I look overhead to see turkey vultures circling. Oak trees are filled with a dozen turkey vultures. I watch the seagull still reigning over the river on his rock. Three ducks swim close. They sit for a while and decide to move on and swim away.

GREAT BLUE HERON MEETS FLIGHT OF CANADA GEESE

WEDNESDAY, OCTOBER 26, 2016, 7:10 AM, 54 DEGREES

WITH SO MUCH CLOUD COVER EACH MORNING, THE MOON IS NOT VISIBLE from the bridge for many days. It is cool and misty outside. I wear a warm, hooded sweatshirt. On my walk to the bridge, I am welcomed by the morning concert from roosters in their usual places – hiding in trees. For the unaware visitor, it appears that trees talk. Without shaking a leaf, the roosters perch on a branch and sing. One lonely and very scrawny chicken emerges from a side street and sings a scratchy song.

Two fishing boats take their places in the river. I see the Egret standing at the end of the boat launch ramp. It arrives about the same time each morning to walk along the riverbank and then flies to search somewhere else for its morning meal.

The bridge rails are covered with moisture. Water drips down in jagged lines to the deck. A turkey vulture flies in. One lone rooster is still crowing. A salmon occasionally jumps high enough to form concentric circles in the water.

I walk to the boat launch ramp to get a closer view of the wildlife and see a salmon take several quick leaps out of the water. The Egret stands at the boat ramp and later flies to the other side. A Great Blue Heron flies in and stands at the boat ramp. A single goose stands nearby. Within minutes, three Canada Geese fly over the bridge honking, honking, and honking. They stretch out their long thin legs and glide gracefully into the water in seconds. After landing, they fold their wings and settle into the water. I watch quietly a few feet away. Geese are now looking and waiting. I watch. I listen. These are the "resident" geese of the river. One of them wears a metal ring around its leg. I have seen this one many times. The Great Blue Heron emits a loud chortle goodbye and flies to the opposite riverbank within a few feet of the Egret. That sudden arrival sends the Egret flying farther east.

NOVEMBER 2016

—

Salmon have returned home to spawn in the American River. Egrets, Canada Geese, seagulls, Great Blue Heron and turkey vultures gather at the river to watch, wait, guard and eat. Chinook Salmon are a critical food source for waterfowl and birds living at the American River.

SUNRISE PAINTS THE SKY FLAMING ORANGE, PINK AND GOLD

THURSDAY, NOVEMBER 3, 2016, 6:50 AM, 48 DEGREES

THE SKY IS STILL DARK WITH ONLY A HINT OF THE APPROACHING DAWN. Roosters crow limply this morning. I walk shining a flashlight all the way to the bridge. *A very misty morning!* The orange glow from the rising sun begins to spread across the sky. After sunrise, glowing white, scattered clouds that resemble spilled milk splash across the sky. They form thin stripes and jagged edges of light. The sky is pale blue in the east and gray to the west. The river is still with hardly a ripple. Mist hangs over the river like a canopy in the distance.

The American River closes to fishing November 1 through the end of the year. Today is my first visit without fisherman lining the river before dawn. Next week, hundreds of salmon will begin their leap into the fish ladder as spawning begins at the Nimbus Fish Hatchery a few miles east.

The bridge deck is striped with water dripping from the truss frame. Few others in the Village are awake yet. One cyclist passes with his headlight flashing and one walker. I feel the vibration of their movements on the bridge before I see them. My fingers are chilled. Three ducks swim quickly to the riverbank.

I find a web spun to perfection between two rails of the bridge. Every line and angle connects precisely as if created with a ruler. The lines are so thin that webs disappears in the light.

One bird flies overhead, then seven honking Canada Geese flying east over the bridge in a "V" formation. When the geese pass, the bridge is quiet again.

A dead salmon floats downstream on the surface of the water. I hear more splashes and see a salmon leap completely out of the water and quickly splash back down. A second and third salmon jump some 20 yards out from the bridge – the same spot where all fishermen sat in their boats to watch and wait. Every minute, another salmon leaps.

Photo shows salmon swimming in front while seagulls watch and wait in background at a shallow and rocky section of the river.

Some salmon jump high enough out of the water to reveal their whole body. Others create ripples and a splash. As the sun rises, more mist forms on the river. The sky is bright and the glowing orange sun rises over the trees. I begin to feel a touch of warmth on my face and see light shining on the bridge rails. My fingers, still cold, I begin walking off the bridge. Something moving in the river catches my eye. A river otter swims toward the bridge from the west. It continues slow and steady movements and finds a small opening in the riverbank about 30 yards on the east side of the bridge.

I watched the otter squeeze into the hole, vanish, quickly reappear and continue swimming around the bend of the bluff. Searching for a distinctive scent? The otter moved on.

Duck morning meeting

SALMON WATCH

Tuesday, November 15, 2016, 2 pm

I WATCH A SERIES OF SPLASHES beginning 100 yards away and getting closer. This shallow part of the river presents the richest experience for watching salmon, seagulls and turkey vultures overhead. A dozen cyclists and walkers also stop to enjoy the salmon navigating the river and the seagulls looking for their next meals.

Hundreds of seagulls line the river, some walk into the rapids, stand, shout and wait. Thirty turkey vultures fly overhead – more than I have ever seen in one place at one time. I watch as a dozen salmon leap,

swim, gather, rest and move on through the rapids to still water.

One dead salmon rests on rocks in the center of the rapids. One at a time, a seagull approaches. It pokes his beak around, pondering what to do and then nibbles on parts of the salmon's underside. One seagull sits in the water near where I stand, open its beak wide and calls to any others who will listen. I watch and listen as seagulls stretch their wings and resettle to stand in the river. A few ducks swim in a quiet pool of water, apparently unconcerned about the activity.

This shallow, rocky section of the river is where I watched ducks search for food in the water a few weeks ago. Now this area is overrun with salmon and seagulls. The arrival of salmon changed the wildlife dynamics at the river. I ride east to another overlook where hundreds more gulls line up and wait. This section of the river is far wider and the only sound is the water moving downstream. Seagulls are silent. No turkey vultures fly overhead. The only clue that this river winds through a suburban community is homes perched on the Fair Oaks Bluff above.

The tip of the thin island where fisherman used to stand is now even smaller. Increased river flows flooded the island so much, it almost disappears. The gulls have overtaken this space as they wait. Turkey Vulture and seagull claim their prize. Neither is willing to share food with anyone.

HAVE YOU EVER HEARD A GOOSE WHISPER?

TUESDAY, NOVEMBER 22, 2016, 6:45 AM, 42 DEGREES

THE SKY IS AWASH WITH SHADES OF PINK FADING IN THE SKY. As the pink turns slowly gray, I see the mist hovering over the water as if this is *Brigadoon* hiding its secrets. The southern sky is woven with pale stripes as the sun rises. The mist gently moves along the river towards the bridge. The movement so gentle it reminds me of fog blowing across a stage in a theater on unseen wind currents.

I wear gloves. My hands feel like ice. The boat launch ramp is empty. A group of four ducks are just now coming out to swim. A single seagull flies west over the bridge. The little bird returned to greet me as it sits at the top of the bridge frame and sing its song, *Ti Too! Ti Too!* Geese fly under the bridge, honking loudly, and land on the west side in their traditional water skiing style.

Runners arrive wearing hats, jackets and gloves. The bridge rails are covered with dew. The deck is moist enough to reveal footsteps. An intact spider web is suspended between two bridge rails. Six dead salmon float next to the riverbank soon to become food for hungry gulls. Canada Geese and turkey vultures monitor the river.

Mornings on Fair Oaks Bridge

I walk to the boat launch ramp and stand alongside two Canada Geese pondering what they will do today. One turns around and spies the river. The other stands and whispers, *Honk, honk* to me over and over. Morning air is so cold, I see its breath form fog clouds as it speaks. What a treat it would be to know geese language. The best I can do is say good morning in *people speak.* The resident Egret is sitting on the north shore in its usual spot.

A single seagull flies over my head. Its circular flight path is 100 yards long, over and over again. The gull is far too high above me to hear the flap of its wings. Yet I do hear its whistle as it circles above six times. The two Canada Geese rise and fly over the river, vanishing into the mist. I leave the boat ramp and walk back over the bridge, giving the river my last glance for the day to hold in my memory. Arriving at my car at 8:10 am, the morning temperature is 49 degrees.

A PLACE FOR PEACEFUL CONTEMPLATION

SATURDAY, NOVEMBER 26, 2016, 7:15 AM, 48 DEGREES

THE GREAT BLUE HERON TREADS CAREFULLY THROUGH THE WATER searching for breakfast. Two seagulls soar over the bridge as I approach. I spy the Egret on the west side looking for breakfast stepping carefully through the water. Even gifted with three long toes to navigate over the rocks and sand, both the Egret and Great Blue Heron walk slowly, contemplating each step. The Egret quietly spreads its wings and flies gracefully across the river to the opposite bank. Two Canada Geese fly in without a sound.

I wear gloves and a jacket. Even in the chill, as my hands and body stiffen, and cool air crosses my face, I find an inner peace and joy from watching the daily activities of wildlife at the river. I marvel at the elegant flight of seagulls, Egret and Great Blue Heron. I listen carefully for distant sounds of Canada Geese approaching and follow their path as they fly over my head. I smile when hearing ducks quacking and complaining. I watch them splashing and chasing each other away. Geese are often the biggest bullies, chasing away anyone getting in their way.

DECEMBER 2016

—————

The exciting mornings watching salmon swim up the river are few now. Seagulls will stay here to feast on salmon and later steelhead through the winter. Instead of crowds of 100 standing in several shallow areas along the river, there are 20 or 30 in one area and a few random sightings elsewhere. Morning temperatures are low. Rain is coming.

NEW VISITORS TO THE RIVER

———

THURSDAY, DECEMBER 1, 2016, 8:25 AM, 42 DEGREES

THE SUN IS HIGH IN THE SKY AND WHITE PUFFY CLOUDS SIT ALONG THE TOP EDGES OF DISTANT TREES. On my way to the bridge, I see two squirrels playing hide and seek as they dance in circles around a palm tree at the curb. Their sharp claws grip the jagged trunk. I hear so much chatter from the tree to my left walking on to the bridge. Small birds chirp, flap and fly from branch to branch. A squirrel darts up and down the trunk. I have seen this squirrel-bird conflict in other trees and wonder if they are naturally unfriendly to each other? *Are birds defending their tree? Are they demanding the squirrel stop shaking the branches as it searches for acorns?*

Ducks are out for a swim. I see ducks fly over; flapping their wings so fast they are a blur in the sunlight. They fly in unison and land at precisely the same moment. I wonder if they are getting flying lessons or just staying busy by chasing each other in the middle of the river? I watch them rise up and fly a dozen feet toward the bridge. Then they chase each other half dozen times, settle into the river, float under the bridge and then disappear.

My fingers are chilled and numb, shaking them every minute to warm up. I look for a sunny spot on the bridge to stand with hopes of getting warm. The east side of the bridge is in shadow where I typically stand watching wildlife activity. The sun is on the west side facing Sunrise Blvd.

Suddenly, it is a busy day at the river! Gulls fly over the bridge in circles and settle in the water. They open their mouths wide and call to each other. I can hear Six Canada Geese honking long before I see them fly in. Ducks continue to chase each other around the river. One seagull calls outs while perched on a rock at the riverbank. Another gull responds from the middle of the river and they continue to call back and forth.

Then all is quiet. I see new visitors to the river. This group of ducks I have not seen before. They swim in the middle of the corridor, floating quietly. They look like they are wearing tuxedos. *Who are these ducks? Where did they come from? I discover these ducks are called Buffleheads.*

MORNING OF STILLNESS

———

WEDNESDAY, DECEMBER 15, 2016, 9:30 AM, 53 DEGREES

USUALLY WHEN I WALK TO THE BRIDGE FROM FAIR OAKS VILLAGE, I listen, look around, and get a "feel" for the morning. Today everything is quiet. Not a single call from chickens. No cars driving on the street. Not a single person walking through the Village. I walk downhill to the bridge entrance and see grass growing on the bridge as green as emeralds. So green, I think about fairies dancing or leaping from the grasses.

As I walk on the bridge, I hear a group of Canada Geese honking loudly on their approach. Geese remain out of sight and their calls fade into the distance. The bridge deck is dark with moisture of the morning. Spider webs washed away from recent rain.

A few people walk. I hear a runner's footsteps, feeling vibrations before he comes into view. Next is the whir of bicycle tires. After several days of rain, the river is swollen with water – sitting at least a foot higher against the riverbank. Folsom Dam is releasing water and the muddy green water flows in ripples quickly downstream toward Sacramento. Ducks are swimming. Buffleheads float in the middle of the river as if they are sleeping. They swim alone. One seagull sits among them.

Salmon run is nearing its end. Steelhead will begin arriving soon. A decaying salmon lies at the end of the boat launch ramp.

Seagull rose out of the water with a splash to fly away
as I snapped the photo.

FEBRUARY 2017

———

So much rain! *Water flows in the Lower American River at Fair Oaks Bridge begin in the High Sierra. Water is released through Folsom Dam and Reservoir, ten miles east, and continues through Nimbus Dam, located less than three miles upriver. Heavy winter storms prompted many huge releases of water. The normally quiet river became a raging torrent with swirling white caps. The flooded river corridor overwhelmed its banks, driving tons of mud and debris 20 miles to its confluence with the Sacramento River at the city's waterfront.*

SO MUCH WATER!

SATURDAY, FEBRUARY 25, 2017, 6:30 AM, 46 DEGREES

I FEEL AS IF I AM THE SINGLE FLOAT IN A PARADE and chickens crowd the streets cheering for me along the route as I walk through Fair Oaks Village. I hear their chants 50 yards away and from one chicken standing alongside a bush a few feet to my left.

The sun has yet to rise in this heavily clouded sky of deep blues and grays. *Thankfully, no rain today!!* I hear the bird that greeted me on the bridge each morning hidden in a tree as I walk past. The American River is still flooded and moving swiftly. Release of water from the Folsom Dam created a raging river. The boat launch ramp and the parking lot behind it were beneath five feet of water only two weeks ago. Parts of the bike trail also flooded and closed. At the time, all I could see was muddy green water, whirlpools and white caps racing downstream. Jim's Bridge vanished under several feet of water. A side fence broke off during the flood and the bridge remains closed. The water has receded and flows a foot below the bottom of the bridge. *Look carefully for the Canada Geese footprints on muddy boat ramp - a leftover from winter floods.*

People walking dogs and cyclists dress in warm jackets and leggings. A chilly wind blows across my face and hands.

Glad to see two geese arrive this morning. They are the first out. They walk alone on the boat launch ramp, still covered in mud and geese prints. Three more geese arrive and land in the water. No gulls, pigeons, birds and not a single duck. A coyote passes me on the bike trail returning to the bridge. He sees me and runs away to hide in the green hills.

Watching muddy water race down the river corridor and under Fair Oaks Bridge displays the impact of too much water coming too fast. Riverbanks are more steeply eroded. Animal homes washed away. I can see part of a yellow sign that has been pushed against the riverbank by raging waters. I read a single word: *"End."*

Flooding along the American River Parkway created this temporary pond.

MARCH 2017

———

Wildlife begins their return to the American River. Visitors see firsthand the impact of flooding. Countless trees uprooted and washed down river are mired in tangles of debris alongside eroded riverbanks. Large ponds form on the American River Parkway in areas traditionally dry. Animal homes and nests were washed away.

WILDLIFE RETURNS TO THE RIVER

FRIDAY, MARCH 3, 2017, 6:45 AM, 41 DEGREES

THE AMERICAN RIVER IS QUIET AGAIN AFTER ONE OF THE WETTEST WINTERS IN 20 YEARS. Birds twitter in distant trees. A wide strip of mud still blankets the boat ramp. The sun rises behind thin, white streaks of clouds. I see a cyclist and a pair of walkers this morning out early.

As I walk to the bridge, I wonder what wildlife has returned to this part of the river.

Half dozen pigeons fly in circles over the bridge three times before deciding to settle down on the truss frame. One flies down and wanders the bridge deck to be joined later by a second pigeon.

As I look out to the water, searching for wildlife, I hear Canada Geese honking immediately behind me. I turn around to see them sitting on a round pier supporting the bridge, discussing what to do next. An instant later, they fly into the sky

still engaged in conversation. Next I check for spider webs attached to the bridge rails and see several perfectly spun webs, with no spiders anywhere. A pair of pearly white Egrets fly in from the west. Their wings spread wide, flapping slowly and gracefully. They are as beautiful in flight as they are to watch after they land. One keeps going and the other stops to rest on the eroded riverbank. No ducks are out swimming today.

The sun has risen high over the trees now. More walkers pass me on the bridge wearing caps, jackets and gloves. A pair of geese approach from the east, flying side-by-side. They fly under the bridge and quickly vanish into the sky. With the riverbank stripped of its vegetation from recent flooding, little food can be found anywhere nearby. Clusters of large spiny, dead branches hold fast. Birds fill the skies. They chirp, twitter and fly from place to place. Their music fills the air as a morning symphony. One bird calls out in a high, shrill voice in a rapid-fire series of *zzz, zzz, zzz.*

My fingers are chilled. The rising sun is beginning to warm the air. A dozen of early morning cyclists whizz by in a hurry. I walk down to the boat launch ramp to see if any ducks are hiding in bushes. I see one duck standing on a patch of dirt directly above the ramp staring out in the distance. It appears to be wondering, *Is it the right time to go for a swim?* I watch as the duck waddles down a short hill to the boat ramp and settles into the water. All the while, *Quack, Quack, Quack.* Then a second duck emerges from the bushes, looking out at the distance just as concerned about swimming as the first one. This duck also waddles down the boat launch ramp to go swimming. They bob their heads in sequence as they swim.

WINTER CHILL LINGERS

—

SUNDAY, MARCH 5, 2017, 7 AM, 43 DEGREES

A GENTLE BREEZE CHILLS THE AIR ON THIS QUIET MORNING. . Only a few chickens are awake this morning after last night's drizzly rain. Birds twitter. Water remains on the streets. Blue gray clouds blanket the sky with faintly different shades of gray.

The bridge is dry, showing no sign of last night's storm. Fair Oaks Bridge is washed clean once again. Spider webs I admired on Friday washed away in the rain. Not even bits of trash, cans or cups litter the deck this morning. Green grass grows in clumps between each deck board.

The yellow "END" sign is still stuck fast alongside the muddy riverbank in a tangle of branches. A large red reflector attached to the signpost is now visible. I wonder if this is the end of the sign's journey down river?

The American River moves quietly downstream with very few ripples as it returns to its pre-rain state. Looking west to Jim's Bridge, I see the water level has dropped several feet below its lower edge.

In response to rain and the chill, the wildlife left the river for grasslands where they can find food. In the fall, ducks played in the gentle rain as if it was not there. Many hide in bushes, keeping warm and guarding nests.

I see the flutter of pearly white wings approaching and recognize the long, sleek bodies as Egrets. They fly over the bridge and continue their journey west. Unlike the Canada Geese I hear hundreds of yards away, the Egrets make no sound at all. They land on an outcropping of land 100 yards west of the bridge.

Few people are out walking yet. *Too cold? Too early?* Even with my warm gloves, my hands are chilled. Cloud cover blocks the sun and its warmth. The bright sky displays no hint where the sun is actually sitting. Two ducks appear. I watch them swim across the river, dive underwater and disappear. They surface 10 yards upriver to dive again. Aside from the twitter of birds unseen in nearby trees, all is quiet at the river.

PIGEONS DANCE AND SEARCH FOR FOOD

Friday, March 10, 2017, 6:45 am, 51 degrees

THE RAIN GONE - SUDDENLY IT IS WARM. TOO WARM! Roosters gather to sing throughout Fair Oaks Village. Warm temperature wakes them early. The American River is as calm as it can be. I see few cyclists or walkers. Two buffleheads swim and dive. A single duck swims. Pigeons dance in circles overhead, then land on the bridge frame. They gather to eat bits of pastry left on the deck and peck at crumbs before rushing back to their stations. The tiniest movements disturb these birds. With a loud flutter of wings, a group of a dozen pigeons fly away in unison, and return as a group to settle down. Why do pigeons seem so nervous?

Unseen birds chatter in rapid succession. A lone goose arrives honking and flies under the bridge, as if speeding through a red light. An Egret flies to a sandbar west of the bridge because its usual spot on the north riverbank washed away during winter storms.

The END sign is gone – I imagine it floated away to some other end on the river.

APRIL 2017

———

Spring arrives and our rainy season is finally over! Wildlife residents near Fair Oaks Bridge search for food along other parts of the river and distant riverbanks. The river at Fair Oaks Bridge is often sadly empty of the ducks, geese and other wildlife often seen here. Melted winter snow races down from the Sierra, causing a wild river.

BUTERFLY AT REST

BEAUTIFUL SPRING DAY! I walk down to the boat ramp where two men prepare to go kayaking. One kayaker is experienced and the other a novice listening to instructions. A lone Canada goose watches and waits for others to join. Few waterfowl have returned since the flood. Two mallards swim in. One Canada Goose joins them. They all linger near the riverbank.

The clear, brilliant green water is moving slowly. Pigeons visit the river. No Egret. No Great Blue Heron. No seagulls. Many cyclists and walkers are out. Few signs of yesterday's rainstorm.

I found a butterfly on the ground on my walk back to the bridge from the boat ramp. It lay flat on the ground kicking its legs. Its rich colors faded. I carefully placed it on the stalk of a plant. It grabbed hold with tiny legs. I wondered if it was going to live. The wind blew gently against its wing. I gently moved the plant. The butterfly adjusted its legs to hold on. Still sitting motionless. I wonder if butterflies sleep?

The American River Parkway is filled with butterflies, flying from one plant to another. A butterfly's life ranges from a few weeks to many months. I hope this butterfly can rest peacefully on the plant instead of being crushed by footsteps.

RIVER OF EMPTINESS – AFTER THE FLOOD

SATURDAY, APRIL 22, 2017, 8 AM

THIN, SCATTERED CLOUDS STREAK THE SKY. The green water is calmly moving downstream. Sunlight sparkles on the calm river. Standing on the bridge, I hear the deep throated cooing from unseen pigeons. The river is empty. Not even one duck is out swimming this morning. All the homes, hiding places, ridges and islands for wildlife to settle on are overrun with water. The river runs high again today and so many once dry places are still flooded.

Tree at left stands with roots exposed as a marker to constantly changing water level. During the peak of winter storms, the tall, thin tree was surrounded by water, sitting as an island several feet from the water's edge. (*see Saturday, February 25, 2017*). Today as in many recent days past, it hugs the eroded shore, roots exposed.

Runners run and a few cyclists cross this bridge, once filled with morning wake up activities, quacks and squabbles, splashes and dives. Today the river is empty. I sit on the bridge and later walk down to the boat launch ramp. No ducks. No Canada Geese. No Egrets. A few birds fly overhead as if to spy on the emptiness of the river.

Several spider webs filled with tiny insects are firmly attached to bridge rails. The sun's bright light reflects on them from all directions.

I hear two geese unseen in the distance for a few seconds before their honking fades away. Today, everything here is quiet. Aside from a few pigeons that settle on the bridge, the only movement here is the river gently flowing downstream. On bike rides and walks along other parts of the American River Parkway, I see Canada geese settle on the sandy banks far inland from the water's edge finding food. A few ducks swim in more shallow areas of the river. The narrow and shallow area where ducks dunk and eat, and salmon spawn, is now expanded to be wide and deep. The river partially covers the adjacent strip of sandy beach.

One of many casualties from the river flooding is this cement memorial bench bearing the quote. *Just another day in paradise,* flipped over on its back. Shrubs, tree branches and other debris pushed down river by the weight of the rushing water still sit in tangles on riverbanks. Leaning branches and uprooted trees remain stranded in the river many weeks after flooding events has eased off.

Jim's Bridge, an access point to the American River Parkway, remains closed and fenced off. The side fences are gone. This is one of my favorite sites to watch flaming orange sunsets spreading light over the sky as if on fire. I have also seen many thrill seekers dive off the edge. For many years, this bridge was a key section for competitors in Eppies Great Race - an annual event where individuals run, cycle and kayak. I eagerly await the return of the wildlife, not knowing if or when they will return to swim and play.

WILD DAY AT THE AMERICAN RIVER

—

SUNDAY, APRIL 30, 2017, 9:30 AM

RAGING WATER FLOODS SANDY BANKS AND ROCKS – popular places for picnics and anchoring rafts. This segment of the American River is called San Juan Rapids because the area is very rocky and usually fairly shallow. Water always moves swiftly here. On this day, the water races down the river channel.

On summer days I sit on a large rock at the water's edge and dangle my feet in shallow water to cool off. Today everything is covered by water. More water will come as melted snow travels down foothills through the Sierra Nevada mountains into the American River.

To my far left, I catch a quick glance at a family of Canada Geese emerging from the rocks and walking into a quiet, shallow area for a swim. I see nine tiny goslings and their parents. *My first sighting of babies this year!* On my way back home, I see a skinny little snake about 12" long in the middle of the bike path. I dragged it to the dirt and the back half of its body wriggled. The top half was still. I think it was near death so I let it lay in peace. Two more skinny snakes sun themselves on the warm pavement – one is dead and the other quickly slithers away as soon as it senses my presence. When snakes leave the grass and move into the bike path to catch some sun they are often run over by speeding cyclists.

A lizard crawls on a rock and stops for pushups as it watches me. Later I see a second lizard on the bike trail. Its life is over. Two Canada geese roam the shoreline at Jim's Bridge, still closed to pedestrians and bicyclists.

I know the waterfowl still roam the banks of the American River after the flood. *Where? When will they return to the area nearby Fair Oaks Bridge?*

MAY 2017

After a long period of hibernation, spring ducklings and Canada Geese swim in the river. Dozens of caterpillars join cyclists and walkers on the bike trail. River is still too wild for rafters, keeping many of them away on Memorial Day weekend – one of the most popular holidays of the year for recreation on the water.

GOSLINGS FIRST SWIM

———

TUESDAY, MAY 9, 2017, 7 AM

GETTING A CLOSER LOOK AT TWO NEW FAMILIES OF CANADA GEESE. I watch goslings tiny webbed feet paddle through the water as fast as they can go. I have seen as many as 70 geese searching the riverbanks and swimming at Jim's Bridge – a far larger number than I have ever seen at one time on Fair Oaks Bridge.

DAILY RITUALS AT FAIR OAKS BRIDGE

THURSDAY, MAY 25, 2017, 7 AM, 37 DEGREES

ONE CHICKEN HIDING IN A TREE CALLS EVERY FIVE SECONDS, over and over and over again. I hear its faint call from the bridge some 100 yards away. *Where is everyone? I am awake!*

Dense clouds float above my head. It is a chilly and windy morning. I have already seen half dozen cyclists and several walkers. A lone boater is in the water and more are preparing to enter the river. The water is calm. Pigeons coo as they straddle the upper bridge frame. Parts of the bridge are covered in spider webs blown apart by winds. After 20 minutes of standing on the bridge, I still hear the chickens calling and the music of birds singing while hidden in nearby trees. Three ducks play in the water at the end of the boat ramp. I hear the distant honk of a single Canada Goose and see it fly under the bridge and continue its west facing flight.

Pigeons are the only ones flying in large numbers this morning. I watch a new family of Canada geese swim over to the riverbank, climb up and disappear into the shrubbery. Even the rocks are laid bare after flooding washed away so many hiding places. Five ducks gather at end of the boat ramp, engaged in their daily cleaning rituals with hardly a sound from any of them. I hear a few soft quacks. It may be too early in the morning to be rowdy and loud.

A tiny feather floats in the air to land softly on the water and drifts away. For the moment, the water is quiet and shimmers. Not a white cap or riffle anywhere. As I prepare to leave the boat launch ramp, an Egret glides through the sky, flying east.

I watch a caterpillar crossing the road slowly twisting back and forth, sensing its next step with roving antennae and moving forward. It crawls over obstacles, pebbles, stones and leaves. The caterpillar keeps moving until it disappears into a patch of green grass.

I see a deer cross the bike trail in front of me. It stops to stare at me hiding behind tall plants.

What is this mark on the ramp? How did it get here?

JUNE 2017

—

Daytime temperatures rise to 100 degrees. Ducks dunk for breakfast bites and relax in morning sun. Water is still wild.

WATERFOWL RETURN AND SEARCH FOR FOOD

—

TUESDAY, JUNE 6, 2017, 7 AM

AIR CHILLED, A SLIGHT BREEZE. SCATTERED, PUFFY WHITE CLOUDS FILL THE SKY.

My morning melody is birds in trees chirping and twittering, combined with the distant buzz of motorcycles and humming cars crossing the Sunrise Blvd. Bridge. Canada geese and ducks are silent and still as they sit on the boat ramp near the water. Some ducks engage in morning clean up rituals. Sunrise was so early this morning the sun is well above the trees before I arrive. Pigeons wander the riverbank cooing and searching for nibbles. No people are here except a few boaters waiting on bites from shad.

Minutes later the geese and ducks wander up the boat launch ramp looking for breakfast. They approach me waiting for handouts.

I ride my bike from the boat ramp to the narrow stretch of beach where the concrete memorial bench is now upright. No waterfowl here. Water is far too deep and fast. I turnaround and ride to the San Juan Rapids, one of my turnaround points on the bicycle trail. The water is deep and very swift. Now all visitors sit and watch.

The American River continues its wild rage as Folsom Dam continues to release water. First we had heavy winter rains that flooded the river. Now we have snowmelt running down from the High Sierra. The river here (and nearly everywhere along the 10-mile stretch I ride regularly) is higher and much wider than usual. The large rock outcroppings and sandy beach area where rafters take a rest stop and families traditionally sit to enjoy getting their feet wet, scenic views and picnic, are all underwater.

Sacramento Bee reported dangerous river conditions on Memorial Day weekend - one of the busiest weekends of the year – kept people away. There were more Canada Geese than rafters.

BOBBIN' FOR BREAKFAST

———

FRIDAY, JUNE 16, 2017, 7:30 AM, 80 DEGREES

ONE HUNDRED CYCLISTS PASS ME RIDING ON THE AMERICAN RIVER PARKWAY. Riding in groups of four to six, they all wore cycling attire with logos. Casual riders pass without bicycle helmets. Fair Oaks Bridge is quiet and filled with spider webs and captured prey. Woodpeckers fly through a dead tree, looking for breakfast. Today will be another scorching day of least 100 degrees. Most Canada Geese (all 70 of them) wander the rocky shore alongside Jim's Bridge. They scavenge the rocks for food and later enter the water for a leisurely swim.

At the boat ramp, geese leave the water to search for breakfast in the dirt. Mallards fly in from the opposite shore. I watch a group of four of them glide into the water straightening their legs to use them as water skis and quickly come to a stop. I watch the action and miss the photos.

Standing close to the water, I watch the Canada Geese and ducks paddle their feet under the water. Each of them bob up and down in the water as they go. Their heads move forward and back. The once tiny goslings are big now. Their characteristic black stripe is darkening on their necks. Four ducks engage in morning cleaning rituals. Three others sleep with their head tucked under their wing. In the distance I hear one lonely chicken call.

Geese pictured at left use their feet to balance while eating breakfast upside down.

RELAXING IN THE MORNING SUN

TUESDAY, JUNE 20, 2017, 7 AM, 70 DEGREES

ON A DAY PREDICTED TO BE 104 OR ABOVE, MORNING ON THE RIVER IS COOL AND QUIET.

Butterflies dance in the air. Birds twitter – *oh eeee, oh eeee.* Cyclists whizz by. Water rushes with rapids forming white caps as they roll over rocks. Hot sun already shines bright. Water glistens with a sunny reflection.

Lizards greet the morning with pushups. Flexing their legs. Watching me. Slinking away. Today I enjoy the stillness of the river. Duck rest on a distant island. Two pigeons rest on the bridge frame. Others choose the cement pier. The headlight of a cyclist flashes as it approaches the bridge.

Canada Geese are in no hurry, relaxing in the warm sun. They swim peacefully through the river toward the boat launch ramp. Tomorrow I will bring grapes to feed them. Birds fly above my head. Cloudless sky. The hot sun melted clouds away. Cool breeze refreshes my skin as I ride. My skin feels hot and sticky standing in one place. Runners, walkers, cyclists come early to enjoy the day before it sizzles.

LIZARD PUSHUPS – A MORNING RITUAL

THURSDAY, JUNE 22, 2017, 6:30 AM, 46 DEGREES

MY FIRST VIEW OF THE AMERICAN RIVER IS WATCHING CANADA GEESE GLIDE LAZILY down the river on the current. Water tinted with shades of blues and greens shimmers in the morning sun. No visible clouds in the deep blue sky. I throw grapes sliced in half to a duck as it watches and waits. The duck not only refuses to eat grapes, it complains about it with a rude quack, as if to say, *Where is the good stuff I can eat?* and waddles away. Farther along the American River Parkway bike trail, a lizard crawls up a tree, around and down again. It climbs on top of rocks, over the ground and then stops for push ups, flexing it legs and watching me. Birds twitter unseen in oak trees. Riding through the Parkway after a rainstorm, everywhere was sparkling green. Now most of the vegetation is dry, gray and weedy. It was only a month ago the water was still flooding the riverbanks. Now the vegetation is bone dry and brown.

FAIR OAKS VILLAGE CHICKENS

Mornings on Fair Oaks Bridge

AMERICAN RIVER PARKWAY PHOTOS

Muscovy Duck on watch at top of Fair Oaks Bridge

Marking a place at the river.

Goose is sitting on concrete bridge support pier.

JULY 2017

———

Turtles have returned to the river, sunning themselves on their favorite branch. A Cormorant hangs its wings to dry on its regular patrols of the Lower American River – including near Fair Oaks Bridge. Woodpeckers stay busy hunting for insects on trees.

CORMORANT AIRS ITS WINGS

MONDAY, JULY 10, 2017, 8 AM

I WATCH DUCKS LAND IN THE WATER AT THE BOAT LAUNCH RAMP. They fly in their typical pattern - stretching out their legs at a slight angle to water ski as they touch the water for one second, then fold their legs and settle their bodies into the water. I see a Cormorant with its characteristic yellow beak and huge wingspan. It flies in regularly to feed and rest along the American River.

Today, the Cormorant arrives on the boat ramp, ignoring all other waterfowl. It stares out into the water, stretches its neck and extends one wing as if hanging it to dry. After a few minutes of airing its wing, it walks back into the river and swims away.

Canada Geese arrive scavenging for breakfast bites. Geese are always the last waterfowl to arrive. Pigeons first, then Mallards, then the geese wake up and show themselves for breakfast. Great Blue Heron and Egrets are far more unpredictable.

At the rocky strip of beach alongside San Juan Rapids, waterfowl rest on newly exposed sandbars. I sit and listen to the gentle sound of water rushing by at this peaceful place. I watch ducks swim in a small area of shallow water as geese stand guard.

TWO TURTLES SUNBATHE AT THE AMERICAN RIVER

——

THURSDAY, JULY 20, 2017, 715 AM, 68 DEGREES

I SEE A COUPLE LOOKING OVER THE SIDE OF THE BRIDGE and ask what they are looking at. They are looking for the beaver eating a whole salmon by stripping meat off the bones. The couple showed me where to look on the riverbank to find its home. They described seeing two river otters and a wayward seal.

I listen to them tell short stories of past times at the bridge: busy young boys who dived from Fair Oaks Bridge into the deep end of the river, speared salmon running wild, and fished from a secret cove. Next, we walked over to view a tree with long, spiny branches hanging over the riverbank and found a turtle sunbathing on a branch. Later that day, I saw the two in the photograph sitting side by side.

Cyclists race by, some stroll past. A few walkers with dogs cross the bridge. Seven Canada geese fly over calling to each other. A passing walker comments on the turtles.

"There used to be 10 turtles. I am surprised any are left after our winter flooding."

A WILD AND BUSY MORNING

SATURDAY, JULY 22, 2017, 7 AM, 68 DEGREES

I HEAR WHAT SOUNDS LIKE A FOGHORN REPEATED THREE TIMES. What is that sound? Where is it coming from? At Jim's Bridge a few ducks are swimming and scavenging. I pass them by and ride my bike on to the boat launch ramp where all is quiet. One woman stands in a boat in the middle of the river and casts her fishing line. Birds greet the morning with songs, even though I cannot see even one. I hear a chorus of tweets and rattles. Pigeons roost on Fair Oaks Bridge.

One Mallard approaches me waiting to receive handfuls of breakfast treats. As it poses for me and waits for a bite to eat, we both hear a quack in the distance. The duck raises it neck and listens for the sound. After a few minutes of waiting for me to throw food and discovering I have none, the duck wanders back into the water.

I see faint wisps of white clouds, as if an artist used a very dry brush on a pale blue canvas. I hear a chicken call from the distance. Calm waters enhance this peaceful scene. Out of the quiet, a cyclist races by, rumbling across the bridge deck.

Half dozen Canada Geese patrol a distant shore. Still no

Egrets arrive. No Great Blue Heron. I search for them every time I come and they are more likely to be where they can find a more plentiful food supply. No sunbathing turtles today hanging out on a branch.

I look for the tall, dead tree on the bike trail where woodpecker families call home. The tree is filled with woodpecker holes from top to bottom. I see a family of four flying from one branch to another, sitting, drumming, joining others, flying off again, sitting in a line.

AUGUST 2017

———

Spectators crowd Fair Oaks Bridge and Fair Oaks Bluff on the day of the solar eclipse. The river has returned to its peaceful state of being. Colorful sunrises further enhance this site's natural beauty. Fishermen begin to gather on the river patiently waiting for the moment when a fish takes their bait.

WILDLIFE AND WONDER

———

WEDNESDAY, AUGUST 2, 2017, 6:30 AM, 78 DEGREES

THE WATER UNDER THE BRIDGE IS SO SHALLOW AND CLEAR I can see the stones lining the river bottom. Two ducks swim in the American River to the boat launch ramp. A group of a dozen young women out for a morning run. A lone boater casts his line. Walkers stroll by.

The sun behind my back feels hot. A gentle breeze refreshes me. Last night clouds scattered across the sky created a golden sunset. This morning the clouds are gone. Two men at the boat launch ramp are throwing seeds to a gathering of a dozen Mallards. The white Pekin Duck follows the others. (Likely a domesticated duck released illegally at the river) The duck pictured limps because its leg is injured. Whenever the duck places weight on its leg to walk, the leg bends and the duck falls. After several failed attempts to walk, it limps back to the water.

A dozen pigeons fly in for breakfast. As is their custom, in a sudden flutter of wings, they rise and fly away. Ducks are still looking for more food searching for any seed fallen deep into the ridges of the boat ramp. One by one they waddle down the ramp and into the water, returning minutes later for another round of searching and eating.

RIVER IN SHADOW

—

TUESDAY, AUGUST 8, 2017, 7:45 PM, 90 DEGREES

SHADOWS APPEAR ON THE RIVER AT TWILIGHT. A few visitors come to walk on Fair Oaks Bridge. Some stop to admire the view. A boater lifts his boat out of the water, preparing to leave the river. As I walk on the bridge, six Canada Geese fly swiftly overhead in their traditional "V" formation. A salmon (presumably) leaps up and out of the water three times. I see only a splash in place of the creature that created the effect.

As the sky darkens with the sunset, no sunlight casts glare down in the water. The river sits in shadows and its colors change to a rich, deep green – similar to that of deep green trees. Water is still. The darkening sky is now tinged with a hazy, gray stripe stretching across the horizon.

I watch four silent ducks swim and disappear under the bridge. Minutes later the ducks have turned around and swim back from where they came. A cool, gentle breeze blows.

The only sound I hear is the wind. Not a bird in the sky. I look out into the water and wonder is that the head of a river otter swimming by? Salmon do not swim with their heads above water. More people arrive, watching slowly and silently. One boat remains in the water at Fair Oaks Bridge. Lights on and equipment ready. Twinkling lights let people know he is still there. Evening air is cools after the sun drops below the horizon. Shadows deepen as the sky darkens and the water loses color and turns darker on the west side of the Fair Oaks Bridge. On the east side, the sun still reflects light, casting long shadows of trees along the shore. The air is still warm. Slowly the scene is almost too dark to see any distinct shapes. Everything is fading into shadows.

PEACEFUL MORNING

—

THURSDAY, AUGUST 10, 2017, 7:15 AM, 68 DEGREES

A DOZEN MALLARDS ON PATROL THE BOAT RAMP TO SEARCH FOR BREAKFAST. As I arrive, they look up and begin to walk toward me. Since I make no throwing motions with food in my hand, they turn around and retreat back down the ramp into the water. A solo fishing boat carries two people. The river is especially beautiful this morning. Many weeks have passed since I have seen it shimmer with so many shades of greens and gold, reflecting trees and sunlight. A pale white moon hangs in the pale, western sky tinged with gray.

Six pigeons fly to their place on the Fair Oaks Bridge frame. The air is chilled. A gentle and cool breeze blows against my skin. This morning my arms were chilled and the car windshield was moist. Sunrise is much closer to 6 am than 5, as it was for so many weeks during the summer. Pigeons feast on remains of a biscuit left on the bridge. At the slightest movement or sound, they flap their wings in unison, fly away and return a minute later to continue their meal. They repeat their flyaway pattern, until they have eaten every crumb they can find. Canada Geese have yet to arrive. Geese tend to be the late sleepers and the grumpiest when it comes to getting their share of breakfast. Ducks retreat to their hiding place.

Soon salmon will be here and fishing boats will multiply by at least five. The river will be standing room only for fisherman standing hip deep in water. I hope seagulls return to feast on the salmon. Maybe the Egret and the Great Blue Heron will return.

I miss the Egrets and Great Blue Heron. Where are the otters and the turtles?

What a delight to see Egret and Heron arrive, walking carefully along the riverbank looking for food and doing their best to avoid each other!

ROCKY REMNANTS OF A FISHERMAN'S ISLAND

―――

FRIDAY, AUGUST 11, 2017, 8:45 AM, 68 DEGREES

SIX CANADA GEESE GREET ME WITH A CHORUS of characteristic honks as I arrive at Jim's Bridge by bike. They join a dozen other ducks already scouting breakfast on the rocky shoreline. True to their nature, the geese are late arrivals for the morning ritual. During a quick trip to the boat launch ramp, I see no waterfowl anywhere. No fishing boats sitting in the American River. I continue my ride east along the bike trail and reach "the narrows." No ducks feeding here today.

Standing at a picnic area far off the bike trail on the river's edge, I watch a Cormorant standing on the rocky remains of what was once an island. It stands motionless on this cluster of rocks for 10 minutes hanging its wings to dry in the early morning air. The bird flies away when its wings are ready. Before the flood, this rocky island sitting in the center of the river channel was large enough for a fisherman to dock his boat, and set out his fishing gear, an ice chest and chair. The water was hip deep. Now all that remains of this island is a small cluster of rocks. At this site on the river, 100 seagull feast on dead salmon during the fall run.

Months after flooding, I still find objects, fallen logs and debris that either float at the surface of the water or have sunk to the bottom.

Clear, shallow water reveals trees washed away by flooding that lay at the bottom of the river.

A signpost pulled out of the ground was swept away and rests on the river floor.

DAY OF THE ECLIPSE

———

MONDAY, AUGUST 21, 2017, 10:15 AM, 72 DEGREES

THE MOON TOOK A BITE OUT OF THE LOWER LEFT PART OF THE SUN at the early stage of 9:15 am. By the time I reached Fair Oaks Bridge at 10:15 am and looked again through a pair of borrowed safety glasses, the sun looked like a sliver – a crescent moon. Sacramento's eclipse reached 77 percent maximum coverage at 10:20 am.

A dozen people gathered outside their offices on Bridge Street. Another dozen people stood on the bridge, watching the sky. At least as many people gathered on the edge of Fair Oaks Bluff hundreds of feet above the American River.

River photo on following page displays an eerie shadow cast on the water with a sliver of visible sun. When the moon passed over the sun, the river became visibly brighter. My excitement over seeing the eclipse was mixed with wonder and sadness when I saw two fire engines – one a special operations unit – idling on the street. Another fire engine sat in the parking area alongside the boat ramp. I was told a spectator standing on the bluff fell off the cliff into the river. Firemen rescued the injured man in a boat. *Photo at right is one of many oak trees perched on the Bluff.*

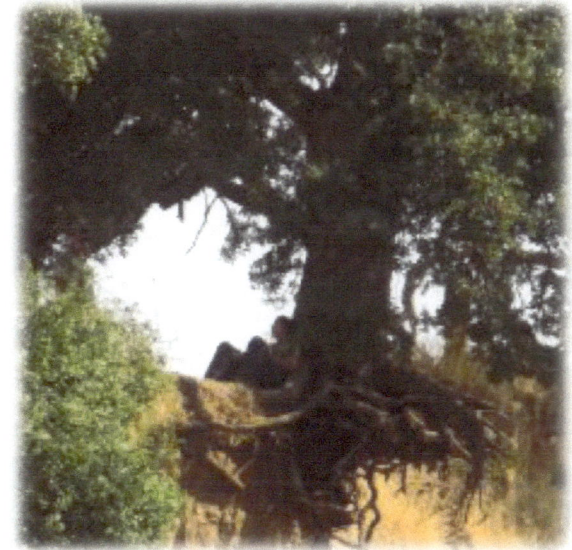

Mornings on Fair Oaks Bridge

CHICKENS GREET THE DAY

WEDNESDAY, AUGUST 23, 2017, 6:30 AM, 65 DEGREES

GOOD MORNING FAIR OAKS! The chickens are singing loudly this morning! Their symphony carries on and on from one tree to another – everyone hiding and singing. This pair took turns listening and singing.

Two early morning hikers slid down the steep trail from the Fair Oaks Bluff nearly falling on top of the surprised and annoyed rabbit in the photo. The rabbit scampers away from the trail to a safer spot near a bush. I imagine the rabbit thinking, *Those hikers falling down the hill was a rude start to my morning!*

I arrive at Fair Oaks Bridge to cloudless sky with a faint smoky haze surrounding the rising glowing, yellow sun. Morning temperatures still feel cool. No breeze blows. The air is still. Last night the air was filled with smoke from area fires. Today all traces of smoky scent are gone.

That mysterious foghorn sounds again this morning. Four chickens scratch and peep on the opposite side of the road. Scratch. Scratch. Looking for breakfast. They walk away after a thorough search. No ducks emerge from the riverbank for their early morning swim. One pigeon arrives to rest on the bridge. Fishermen sit in their boats sit and wait. Some roam to the opposite side of the bridge for a better position.

I feel the sun heating up the air as the sun rises higher over the trees. The air feels heavy already. A few individual walkers and a lone cyclist are out. Reflecting like a mirror, the clusters of trees on the Fair Oaks Bluff west of the bridge cling to the riverbank.

Where is the small bird that used to land on the overhead frame of the bridge last fall? It sang its good morning song each day I visited the bridge. I have yet to see or hear it.

A group of four ducks swim under the bridge. Another straight line of four ducks swim by. One sounds a morning call, *Quack...Quack...Quack.*

IN THE MOMENT OF SUNRISE

SUNDAY, AUGUST 27, 2017, 6:15 AM, 72 DEGREES

SUNRISE IS A FLAMING GLOW FILTERED BY HEAVY CLOUD COVER. Clouds begin to spread as the sun rises. A lone fisherman watches and waits. A gentle breeze blows on my warming skin. The morning chicken symphony is long and loud. A large white chicken surprises me with its call from a tree branch directly above my head. I watch a pair of ducks lazily floating under Fair Oaks Bridge. They look around and float with the current, with no effort. Another pair floats the opposite direction. One pair must be paddling, since the current flows in one direction.

The sun's rays are glowing through heavy cloud cover. Three boats take their places on the river. Two fishermen stand in the middle of the river waiting for their catch of the day. Leaving the bridge 7:15, morning air feels hot and heavy – it is 81 degrees.

SEPTEMBER 2017

———

Salmon are on their way! Fishermen line the river before dawn for the joy and excitement of landing salmon swimming up the river to spawn. A chill fills the air. Fall has arrived.

MUSIC OF THE MORNING

———

SUNDAY, SEPTEMBER 3, 2017, 6:20 AM, 74 DEGREES

CHICKENS SING SONGS IN HARMONY TODAY.
Each chicken is still hidden away for the night in tree branches and crowing without end. *I am certain the two chickens pictured believe they are still hiding.* The morning sunrise is barely visible behind clouds. A cool breeze blows – The air is already too warm for so early in the morning.

Three cyclists rumble the bridge as they pass. I see one turn his head to the left and looks to the American River. Five boats sit in the river and another boater arrives at the boat ramp. As the boater prepares his gear for launch, the wind carries the voice of John Denver on a CD singing *Born a Country Man.*

A pink sunrise spreads across the sky and changes colors, reflecting on thick white, puffy clouds. The hot orange sun rises above the trees. Another hot day is coming. At 7:10 am, the temperature is already 82 degrees.

WHAT SOUNDS GO UNHEARD?

—

FRIDAY, SEPTEMBER 8, 2017, 6:35 AM, 64 DEGREES

IS THIS MORNING CHILL A SIGN OF MORNINGS TO COME? My mornings of wearing shorts, a t-shirt and sandals are certainly to become less frequent. Chickens that provide daily wake up calls in Fair Oaks Village are still slumbering. I always hear the chickens; and always listen for the ducks and Canada Geese. Birds hiding in trees greet the day with a melody. The pigeons on the bridge sound off every morning. Occasionally I hear the chortle of a Great Blue Heron. *I wonder what other sounds are held in the morning air that I am not hearing*?

River is shallow enough here at the boat ramp to see the rocky bottom. Ducks engage in morning cleaning routines.

The glowing yellow sun emerges in the eastern sky over the heads of trees lining the American River. As I sit quietly and listen for sounds, I hear the call of one Canada Goose, a honk and then silence. I wonder how far away is it? How fast is it flying?

Our fifth year of drought that ended with heavy rain and flooding, leads me to wonder, what is usual and customary on the river? How will activity on the river change this coming fall? Will the waterfowl return? How many salmon will come? Will wildlife return to feed on the salmon as they did last fall?

Four ducks emerge from hiding and swim under the bridge heading west. They swim past fallen trees lying on the river bottom, yet visible in the clear, shallow water. The ducks pass trees with exposed roots along the eroded riverbank. Flooding and erosion over time caused many of the prominent features along the river corridor – such as the tree in this photo, clinging by its roots to the riverbank.

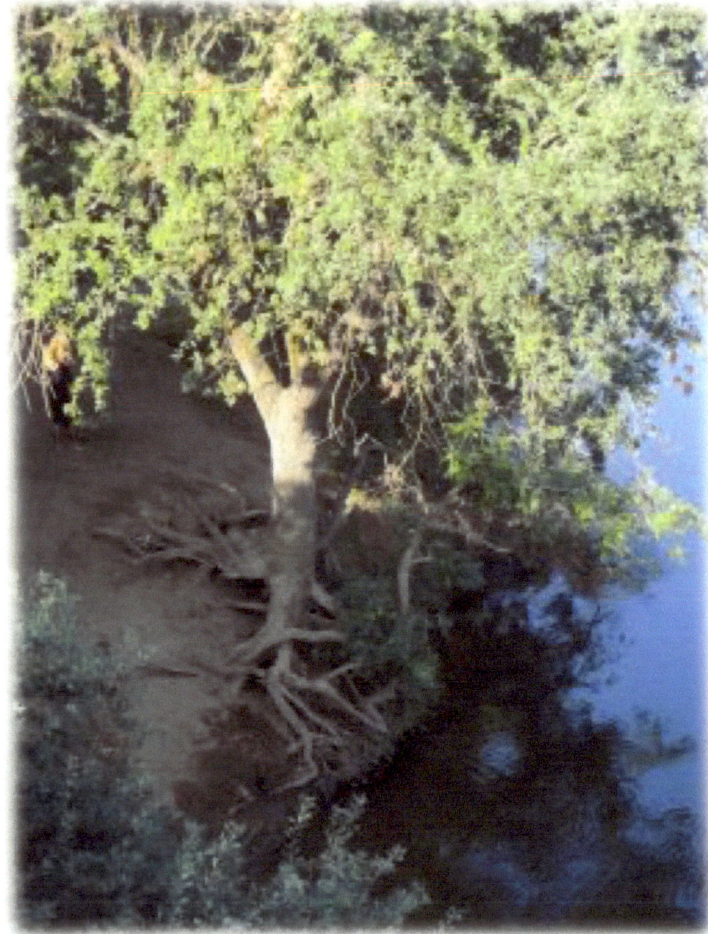

REFLECTIONS ON WILDLIFE

———

Sunday, September 10, 2017, 6:30 am, 65 degrees

A CROWD OF CANADA GEESE AND DUCKS are swimming at Jim's Bridge, engaged in morning rituals and scavenging for breakfast. They hang out on the south side of the riverbank. They poke at the rocky shore and swim in shallow water, looking for worms, insects and other morning nibbles.

I arrive at Jim's Bridge and all the waterfowl are here! The abandoned Pekin duck has joined the Mallard families. *Quack! Quack! Quack!* The ducks are quietly waking up, swimming, cleaning, quietly poking their head into the water searching for a morning meal. Occasionally one duck will rant, *Quack! Quack! Quack! Quack! Quack! Quack!* and no one pays attention. The geese and the ducks pictured below are expecting a morning handout.

Mallards are so unlike chickens that call out to each other all day long, and call when no one is there to hear. When I hear ducks voice their opinions, few others respond until they squabble at feeding time.

In a moment, three ducks rise and fly quietly to the opposite shore. Watching them gives me a chance to take a breath and feel the chill on my skin. I look up to see 20 birds sitting on power lines above the Sunrise Blvd. Bridge.

Mornings on Fair Oaks Bridge

Daytime temperatures are warming already. I ride my bike to Fair Oaks Bridge. The parking lot for the boat launch ramp is filled with pickup trucks and utility vehicles equipped to tow their boats. I count seven boats in the river, all on the east side of the bridge. There are almost as many fishermen on the American River as there are ducks.

A mother duck swims with her two young ducklings. They move past the boats, leaning trees and those uprooted and fallen into the river. They pause their morning a few moments before moving on. Many birds twitter while hidden in trees. Sometimes when I find feathers on the ground. I pick them up and wonder how do birds or the chickens lose their feathers? Was it a battle or an argument? Or losing this feather was a natural part of growth.

I believe that ducks, geese and birds may exercise far more patience than people. People are often in a rush to get anywhere – pack in as much into the day as possible before dropping off to sleep or not even sleep. Waterfowl take their time to swim, play, and clean their feathers.. A duck's days are for sunning, sleeping, eating, relating to other ducks - and staying away from predators and Canada Geese bullies.

I sit here and wonder what is my role in helping to preserve this peaceful spot where wildlife can thrive? I remain surprised at how many visitors here pass through without noticing the abundance of life that resides here.

WONDER AND JOY

—

SUNDAY, SEPTEMBER 10, 2017, 8:40 AM, 65 DEGREES

EACH DAY IS A MIX OF WONDER AND JOY! I arrive at Fair Oaks Bridge after a bike ride on the American River Parkway. I rode to the San Juan Rapids one mile or more downstream to the west. I stop to enjoy the view at my farthest destination for the day. No wildlife here, no people, cyclists pass.

Rivers are complicated. They provide so many benefits and serve so many needs. By regulating flow levels, the river can meet the needs for healthy habitats and retain water quality for all. As I arrive at the bridge, I continue to see cyclists pass. One carries a small dog tucked inside her sweatshirt. Others walk dogs, large and small. Many people walk on the bridge and few pause for even a moment to look to one side or the other.

I marvel each morning at the scenic panorama and mysteries of this natural world. This feeling of wonder and joy seems lost on many others. I engage in conversation with visitors who stop to watch and take photos. I ask them when they come and what they see to learn more about the river and its history.

Duck pictured is searching the shallow river bottom for tasty treats.

MORNING OF PEACE

MONDAY, SEPTEMBER 11, 2017, 6:20 AM, 72 DEGREES

ENJOYING THE SERENITY OF THE MORNING ON FAIR OAKS BRIDGE, I pause to reflect on this time, day and peaceful setting - remembering that people across the nation gathered in parks and open spaces searching for their own inner peace as they struggled to cope with the tragic events and losses on 9-11-2001.

I arrive at the bridge as morning light is still filtered by shadows. A single chicken calls good morning. A cool breeze blows. The air feels crisp, even at 72 degrees. The sun is emerging. A scattered orange glow of excitement for the new day spreads across the sky.

As tired as I sometimes feel in the morning, the cool air, sight of radiant sunrises, touch of cool breezes and scenic views of Fair Oaks Bluff are ways to wake and find inner peace.

The American River is so still, the vibrant landscape of Fair Oaks Bluff reflects as a mirror on the west side of Fair Oaks Bridge.

Mornings on Fair Oaks Bridge

A single fisherman arrives as two others prepare to launch their boats. One fisherman paddles lazily up the river. Many walkers are out early this morning. Three Canada Geese fly silently high over the bridge heading west. One chicken continues its solo. Birds sing hidden in the distance when the chicken pauses its song. They watch and wait. I finally hear the first quack of the morning, although the duck remains invisible. Several ducks emerge and swim under the bridge. A group of eight Canada Geese fly over the bridge. I hear them honking long before seeing them. Birds sing all around me. More people are out walking as the day brightens. Cyclists ride by with headlights flashing. Twenty pigeons straddle the huge truss frame of the bridge. A sparrow quickly joins them. I hear birds whistling and Canada Geese flying in a "V" formation above my head to disappear as they move south.

Fall is approaching. I wonder what interactions will be next? I will be looking for the gathering of 100 seagulls farther upriver where salmon spawn. I will be looking for the crowd of hungry turkey vultures hovering in trees waiting for the dead salmon to float in the river.

As the sun continues to rise above trees on the eastern shore, the orange glow changes as light is filtered through the clouds. An airplane draws a jet stream across the sky. More geese fly in from the west. Duck pictured at right is taking a break and leads me to think of morning meditation.

DIVERSE WILDLIFE WAIT FOR SALMON

―――――

FRIDAY, SEPTEMBER 15, 2017, 6:30 AM, 62 DEGREES

WHAT A BEAUTIFUL MORNING! The sun casts a pale orange glow behind clouds that stretch across the eastern sky in wisps. Cool, moist air creates dew on my windshield. I wear jeans and two layers of shirts for the first time.

Three boats sit in the river a few yards away from Fair Oaks Bridge. Passengers of each one engage in conversation across the water. Today I see more boats on the river than waterfowl.

Ducks greet the morning with their persistent quacks. Pigeons sit in their usual spot. Other birds join them. I see the Great Blue Heron return to the boat launch ramp this morning. It stands watching the river, rises up with a chortle and flies to the opposite riverbank. A few minutes later, it returns to the south side of the river. This time landing at the riverbank a few yards from the bridge. It walks the edge until I can no longer see it. I suspect this arrival at 6:30 will become a morning ritual. I wonder what the Great Blue Heron will find to eat this morning?

Diverse wildlife returning to Fair Oaks Bridge is another sign of a changing season and the expectation that salmon will be arriving soon.

Fishermen stand in the American River up to their hips during the chill of early mornings waiting for fish to take their bait.

Mornings on Fair Oaks Bridge

It amazes me that fishermen can rise long before dawn to launch their boats and sit or stand for hours on the river waiting for a tug on their fishing pole. A group of Mallards emerge from hiding to greet the passengers.

> *I wonder how the winter rain, flooding and disruption of habitat will impact this year's salmon run? Will there be enough salmon to feed the wildlife, supply the fisherman, and all the other places where people eat salmon? I continue to wonder about the long-term survival of the salmon with so much other life depending on them.*

Two Canada Geese fly swiftly overhead. I imagine they plan to travel long distances because they are so much higher in the sky than I usually see them. Others fly over and maneuver in the air – soaring downward and losing altitude, then rising again. Some geese turn and fly into the water for a splash landing. Others quickly fly away and disappear. Canada Geese have been absent from the river lately. Usually they are late arrivals.

A cyclist passes me. He looks sideways and says, *Beautiful*, and races away.

A loud noise causes 30 pigeons to react by fanning their feathers and flying into the sky, circling the bridge and vanishing. I have yet to discover why pigeons are so nervous, or why they fly in circles only to land again moments later. I can only guess this is a morning ritual. Very few pigeons spend their afternoons on the bridge. Still the day is extraordinarily quiet. Water level of the river is very low.

By 7:20 am, the sun has risen above the trees on the south shore. I feel its warmth walking off the bridge. I catch a shadow of the bridge and myself standing on it reflected on the trees growing on the north riverbank. In two minutes, the scene changes when the sun rises higher and the shadow vanishes.

BEAVERS SWIM AT DAYBREAK

——

Monday, September 18, 2017, 6:25 am, 60 degrees

AT 6:30 AM, THE BRIDGE IS CROWDED WITH PEOPLE! Six bicyclists cross Fair Oaks Bridge shortly after I arrive. Morning temperatures drop into the 50s and 60s. I wear blue jeans, and a lightweight denim jacket and sneakers. A light breeze blows and I feel the air heavy with chill instead of the heat that roasted our air all summer long.

Three fishing boats sit in the river wait quietly. One person caught a fish. Fishermen catch the early arrivals. Water level of the American River is the lowest I have seen all year. Reduced water flows improve spawning habitat.

Pigeons take their stations on the overhead frame. The tiny bird greets me with *Ti Too! Ti Too!* from its place at the top of the bridge. Two more groups of Canada Geese fly over. Thirty runners cross the bridge together out for an early morning sprint.

My first time seeing a beaver swimming in the river! I walk to the north side of the bridge to follow it and see two more. Two photographers join me this morning. They point out a man climbing down the slope of Fair Oaks Bluff. *Why? How?* We have no idea.

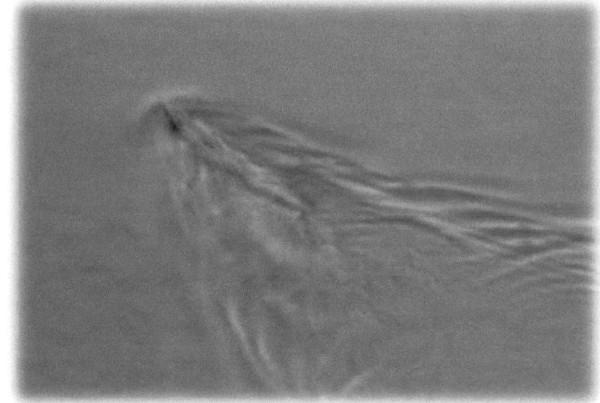

MORNING RITUALS OF FALL

FRIDAY, SEPTEMBER 22, 2017, 6:35 AM, 55 DEGREES

NOT A CHICKEN IN SIGHT AS I DRIVE INTO FAIR OAKS VILLAGE. Yet the morning symphony is as loud and as long as ever. I wonder if cool temperatures wake chickens earlier, inspiring them to begin calling each other. The brutal 100-degree days of summer are behind us. Today's temperature is a dramatic change from two weeks ago when morning temperature was 72 degrees at 6:30 am.

My first sight at the bridge is the line up of eight boats stationed in their places on the American River. A group of four Mallards swim past the boats, ignoring them altogether. More than 40 pigeons circle the bridge a few times and then settle in their usual places.

As I stand and watch the sunrise, I spy a Great Blue Heron fly in and land on the boat launch ramp. I remember from last fall, the ramp is the heron's first stop at this part of the river. The Heron stands and watches the sky, pondering its next move. With a chortle, this beautiful bird rises up and flies across the river to patrol the other side. The Great Blue Heron flies again after a few minutes of walking gingerly along the riverbank. Its next stop is the river's edge directly beneath the bridge, where it continues to patrol and go out of sight. This is a morning ritual each time the Heron appears. I watch it closely to track its movements. At a distance, the color of its body blends into the background.

From the bridge, I watch an Egret land on the boat launch ramp and walk along the riverbank. I arrive at the ramp in time to watch it rise, spread its wings and slowly, gracefully fly away into the western sky. A single goose and two ducks approach me, anticipating breakfast is coming. None comes. They quickly swim away. More ducks fly in and settle on the river to begin morning rituals.

Standing on the boat ramp, I watch a dozen cyclists rumble across the bridge causing dozens of pigeons to rise and fly off the bridge to resettle after the disturbance has passed.

Some fishermen arrive before dawn and leave soon after sunrise. Others stay and bring their breakfast on board, enjoying morning hours on the river waiting for salmon to bite. Some fishermen cook breakfast on portable barbecues in their boats. The owner of the boat at right cleaned his salmon at the river's edge before bringing his boat up to the ramp.

Mornings on Fair Oaks Bridge

VIBRANT SUNRISE

———

Friday, September 29, 2017, 6:30 am, 60 degrees

AN EGRET STANDS AT THE END OF THE BOAT LAUNCH RAMP searching for breakfast. In minutes, it flies away. A duck quacks. I hear the chortle of the Great Blue Heron out on the river that I cannot see because its deep blue-gray wings blend in with the gray morning light.

As dawn turns into daylight, the pigeons fly in to take their places. The tiny bird arrives as the sun rises over the trees – a cool breeze blows on my face. The little birds sings its morning song, while enjoying a panoramic view.

Standing in awe of the sunrise, I see and hear a splash. A proud fisherman catches a salmon. I see it thrashing wildly in the net.

At dawn two groups of Canada Geese fly over high in the sky for a long flight. My hands are chilled. Cyclists and runners pass dressed in warm clothing. It is nearly 7:30 am when people arrive for walks on the bridge. Later, a group of 20 cyclists riding together cross the bridge.

OCTOBER 2017

———

Wildlife of American River wait for salmon to arrive – seagulls, Great Blue Heron, Egrets, ducks, Canada Geese, and Turkey vultures. Seagulls sit in flocks of 100 in shallow areas where salmon swim upriver and stop to spawn.

MALLARD SPEAK

SUNDAY, OCTOBER 1, 2017, 6:30 PM, 72 DEGREES

A BEAUTIFUL FALL EVENING CAPPING A WARM, BREEZY DAY – a fragment of stronger winds of earlier today. A year ago, the island pictured was large enough for fisherman to dock their boats, bring a folding chair and ice chest. Since the flood, this strip of land is barely enough for Cormorants to stand on.

Standing on the bridge I see an Egret return to the riverbank. It huddles on the north side. Egrets and Great Blue Herons are almost always alone. I wonder why?

I rarely see Mallards alone. Even the domestic white Pekin duck, likely released into the river by a family, joins the crowd. Several Mallards speak, arguing loudly in duck speak language that I do not understand.

Pigeons repeat their circles near the bridge. Once, twice, three times before they settle and quickly depart for another destination. All is quiet on American River today. One fishing boat sits. The eastern sky resembles an artist palette of pale blue, tinged with gray at the horizon, and pinks and white stretching across the sky.

I hear a splash in the water. What was it? I am not fast enough to see if it was a salmon, beaver or otter? Usually, salmons are the noisy ones. Otters and beavers surface and vanish with hardly a ripple. Six ducks fly under the bridge and I miss photographing their landing.

A pink sunset spreads across the horizon and I watch the blurred edges of dusk transform the landscape into dark shadows.

This photo shows the narrow, shallow area of the river looking west (downstream) where visitors can see the best viewing of salmon swimming upstream and others spawning in the shallow water.

WHERE SALMON SWIMS, SEAGULLS FLY

SUNDAY, OCTOBER 15, 2017, 7 AM, 46 DEGREES

MORNINGS ARE MUCH COOLER. I AM SURPRISED IT HAS NOT RAINED YET. Usually it rains the weekend we decorate our home with outdoor Halloween decorations. I wear jeans, long sleeve shirts, long socks, and a jacket or sweatshirt on my morning visits. My hands are chilled. I have yet to put my gloves on. Mist covers my windshield and the moist air stays on. Despite the cold, people are out walking their dogs.

*This morning, as all mornings, the same small, skinny chicken calls out "I am awake" in chicken speak
and scratches the dirt to find breakfast. I can hear it call as long as I stand on Fair Oaks Bridge.*

Two young adults huddled in a blanket engage in vibrant conversation as they point to photos in an album propped up in their laps. They continue to review photos without looking up. When I arrive a cluster of fishermen sit in boats on the American River as if they were holding a conference. Fishermen return to this site east of Fair Oaks Bridge, year after year to fish, to share fish stories and brave the chill of early mornings for the thrill of catching salmon. I have not anyone how many days a week they come to the river?

Today I see my first seagull of the season landing near the boat launch ramp. I smell the faint scent of dead salmon in the air. As November draws closer, seagulls know food is plentiful here and they wait.

Two hungry turkey vultures fly overhead - another clue that salmon have returned to the river. The seagull takes flight and glides through the air toward the bridge, scanning the water. After circling twice, it vanishes. Far more food lies about half a mile upriver. I wonder if the seagulls will be there yet?

A dozen pigeons approach and land on the bridge. I expect to see far more salmon jumping and splashing. I see only a few in an hour. A Cormorant flies under the bridge headed west. I follow its flight close to the riverbank and then lose sight as it blends into the distant landscape. Moments later, this elegant bird returns to circle the bridge.

I watch a seagull float gracefully over the bridge and land in the river near the boat launch ramp. Unlike ducks that splash down with wings spread and feet extended as if water skiing, seagulls land sitting down, wings tucked in without a ripple. When I hear the seagull call, I wonder is it calling for others to join? Asking where is the food? Or locate its flock? Immediately afterwards, one lonely chicken calls from Bridge Street. *Where else can you hear the call of a seagull and the rousing good morning from a chicken in the same place and time?*

Seagulls and other resident wildlife of the American River are anxious for salmon to arrive.

SEAGULL STANDS GUARD

———

WEDNESDAY, OCTOBER 18, 2017, 7:45 AM, 75 DEGREES

SEAGULL ENJOYS A SALMON FEAST. Walking down to the sandy shore at San Juan Rapids overlook, I found two seagulls perched on a small island at the edge of the water. One seagull fiercely guards a dead salmon. Occasionally, the gull pulls a nibble off the badly decayed fish, as if it were its luncheon plate. Five yards away sits another gull, alone, watching without food. I wonder what this second one could be thinking? I watch seagulls stand in the water as salmon swim past them. What could they be thinking? *Hey! Another one got away!*

The winds shift suddenly and the air carries the smell of rotting salmon. The familiar scent has brought vultures to check out the scene. Two circle in the pale blue sky, set against of background of blue and gray puffy clouds. I see a flock of Canada Geese fly in 100 yards downriver and take their places along the riverbank. Two Mallards swim by me. More seagulls arrive to float on the water.

How can there be so much salmon and I see so few of them jumping out of the water? Some not interested in making the leap?

A decayed salmon lies in the water as the seagull stands guard over his feast.

FLIGHT OF SEAGULLS

———

SUNDAY, OCTOBER 22, 2017, 1:15 PM

One of my favorite viewing spots to see seagulls waiting and salmon jumping is about a mile east of Fair Oaks Bridge. A paved road leads off the bike trail to a picnic area overlooking the river. I often visit here to watch the fishermen, seagulls and ducks at play. Today when I arrived, I saw a fisherman walking toward me carrying a large salmon in his net that I estimate weighed about 25 pounds.

Thirty seagulls gather on an island in the center of the river. All waiting and watching for a tasty salmon meal. Last October, I counted 100 seagulls gathered here. Today a dozen turkey vultures circle over my head. I only see vultures flying overhead during the salmon fall run.

Suddenly all the gulls flapped their wings and lifted into the sky. They flew so high, they looked like glittering white stars.

Seagulls flew in wide circles for two minutes until the entire flock flew west and vanished. A dozen returned minutes later. A dozen Canada Geese flew in, honking loudly and landed with a loud splash close to the north riverbank. A single fishing boat floats in the water. Occasionally, I hear a *plop* as a stray salmon lifts its head above water and quickly falls back down.

CANADA GEESE ON PATROL

——

FRIDAY, OCTOBER 27, 2017, 7:30 AM, 54 DEGREES

MY FIRST SIGHT AS I WALK ON THE BRIDGE IS A GREAT BLUE HERON standing at the end of the boat ramp. I walk to there for a closer look and approach quietly so I don't give it reason to fly away before I arrive. Standing at the top of the ramp, I take this photo seconds before a young man in his snapping flip-flops rushes toward it as if in a trance.

The Great Blue Heron heard the snapping sound and responded with a chortle that I imagined to be, *I am getting away from this disturbance* and flew to the opposite riverbank. Standing in the same spot as the heron, the intruder stares out into the distance for one minute. He walks across the boat ramp, stares again, walks silently walks back to his car.

Moments later, Canada Geese flew in and walked up the ramp, beaks to the ground, searching for something to nibble on. They marched slowly in line across the driveway leading down to the boat ramp. They reminded me of *the geese patrol* on a hunt for breakfast.

MOMENT TO MOMENT EXPERIENCES

———

SATURDAY, OCTOBER 28, 2017, 7:20 AM, 52 DEGREES

WHY DO BOATS LINE UP ON THE EASTERN SIDE OF FAIR OAKS BRIDGE? Seven boats sit in line on the American River (from east to west). Fishermen always anchor their boats on the north side of the river. Is the water level deeper on that side? The south side where the boat launch ramp is located tends to be shallow almost half way out.

Two walkers pass. An older man calls out to me, "It is cheaper to buy salmon at the store than to go fishing in the cold. It is freezing out there on the water." I turned and replied, "Then you miss the experience. You cannot buy the experience."

It is a rare opportunity when I can ask fishermen why they venture into the cold river before dawn to catch salmon. For devoted fishermen, catching a wild salmon, watching it jump and wriggle and try in vain to escape is the thrilling culmination of a fishermen's joyful anticipation and planning. Some salmon get away. Their struggle to escape can be stronger than the fishing line. At the final moment after catching the salmon, skillful hands cannot hold the thrashing fish. The salmon wins to fight another day.

I watch the fishermen as they find the best spot and cast their lines. They share fish stories and talk across the water to other fishermen in nearby boats. Many arrive before dawn and eat breakfast on portable grills. These are experiences that no one can buy in a store.

I have visited this part of the American River more than 100 times and I still marvel at the beauty of this place.

I return to watch the ducks swim by, creating their own small wake in the river. Next I see a circle of pigeons flying above the bridge. Canada Geese swim under the bridge. An Egret flies and lands on the boat launch ramp. Ducks are busy finding breakfast on the boat launch ramp and under the water. I remain in awe how various species of birds take flight and land, using their wings and feet in different, yet very precise ways. Ducks dunk and stay upside down for two minutes searching for food underwater. They paddle their feet to keep them balanced. When ducks come up, they float a while and dunk two, three or four times before moving on to the next spot.

Many waterfowl gather to feed on salmon. I don't smell the scent of their decaying bodies as much as I have in the past. Two dead salmon lay at the river bottom below the bridge.

I stand and watch a series of circles in the water created by Canada Geese who rise and flap their wings in the air for 20 yards before ever lifting out of the water and rise into the sky. I listen to the sound of the tiny bird, *Ti Too. Ti Too* as it rests on the truss of Fair Oaks Bridge.

FEAST AT THE AMERICAN RIVER

TUESDAY, OCTOBER 31, 2017, 1:30 PM, 70 DEGREES

TODAY IS THE LAST DAY OF FISHING FOR THE YEAR. Tomorrow salmon can swim undisturbed up the river to their spawning grounds. All of them will stop when they reach the weir at Nimbus Fish Hatchery. Some will lay eggs in the river. Many will climb the fish ladder into the hatchery for spawning.

It is late in the day, so the morning fishermen have left the river. Two boats sit in the water. Seagulls patrol the sky. A dead salmon lies on the shallow bottom along the river. I am surprised to see a Great Blue Heron walking along the riverbank on the west side of the bridge. An early morning stroll at 6:30 am is far more common. I walk along the American River Parkway to a shallow, rocky area (now much wider after that flood) and see a seagull enjoying his meal. Twenty seagulls sit and wait.

During this time of year, it is difficult to capture everything I want to remember in writing and photographs. Four turkey vultures circle, dozens of seagulls call, and other waterfowl swim peacefully. Two salmon swim forward and then another. The easiest way to spot a salmon swimming is to watch for the flip of its tail. Water splashes and one salmon rises to the surface. Salmon are barely visible because their dark colors blend in with the color of the water. Each one that passes

rises to the surface of the water for only a second before its swims down below again to continue on this last part of its long journey from the Pacific Ocean. I see a third salmon flip its tail and disappear. In 45 minutes, I see six salmon swim past me. Certainly many more stay under the water where no can see them.

Photo shows an Egret vigorously shaking the salmon, expecting it to break apart into smaller pieces and become easier to swallow.

Using its beak is not working, so the Egret throws the salmon to the ground to dunk it under the water. The salmon remains whole. The Egret resumes shaking the fish. Again nothing happens. Finally the Egret decides to chew on the whole salmon a little more. The Egret tires of tearing up the dead salmon and flies to the opposite riverbank for privacy after several minutes of frustrating efforts.

I notice during these morning visits that all larger birds – Egret, Great Blue Heron and even the Turkey vultures tend to stay in the background, waiting their turn. They go on patrol individually. The Turkey vultures get rid of competition by spreading their large wings to warn others of their kind that this is their territory and/or their catch, In essence, *"Scram! Go find your own fish!"*

A rare moment to see the Egret (left) and Great Blue Heron (right) stand together with seagulls in a shallow part of the river to feast on dead salmon. Some seagulls prefer standing alone or in groups to watch salmon pass.

NOVEMBER 2017

—

Seagulls and other waterfowl are still feasting on salmon. They roam the river through many mornings of thick fog. A heavy mist blankets Fair Oaks Bluff and rolls slowly under Fair Oaks Bridge. Sunrise through fog illuminates trees along the bike trail.

GULLS CALL AND DUCKS SQUABBLE

FRIDAY, NOVEMBER 3, 2017, 7:50 AM, 57 DEGREES

DRAMATIC CLOUD COVER BLANKETS THE SKY AND SENDS DOWN A GENTLE RAIN. Random patterns of drops fall on streets, sidewalks and the deck of Fair Oaks Bridge.

All fishing is over until January. Spawning salmon and other creatures of the American River are left at peace. On this quiet morning, white clouds blanket the sky in thick round rolls covering a pale blue backdrop. A gentle breeze blows leaves of gold, red and orange from nearby trees into the river and they float lazily under the bridge.

Mallards gather at the boat launch ramp for a morning meeting. I hear the chortle of a Great Blue Heron from the ramp. It rises up and flies in to sit about 30 yards from me. Although I hear it clearly, the pale blue colors blend in with the landscape and the heron remains unseen. A Turkey Vulture flies over my head, scans the river and continues to fly west. Four more Mallards fly in with fluttering wings and a splash – their legs stretched out straight ready for a "ski in" landing.

Two seagulls call out to each other. I continue to wonder what they are saying. Could it be *Where is the food? Where is the flock? I am hungry!* Or *Get breakfast here.* I watch each gull open its mouth wide and tilt its head back. The sound comes from deep inside their throat.

GENTLE RAIN

———

THURSDAY, NOVEMBER 9, 2017, 7:15 AM, 55 DEGREES

LAST NIGHT'S RAIN WASHED THE AIR CLEAN. I see sharp clear lines on the trees, landscapes and structures. Even after the rain has come and gone, I still see spider webs clinging to side rails of the bridge. Today the air feels like a crisp fall day. White billowy clouds cover the sky. River is still and seems empty of wildlife so far.

As I stand on Fair Oaks Bridge, the small bird that favors its observation post at the top of the frame calls out a good morning greeting. Other waterfowl have not arrived yet.

By this time of year, I expect to see many salmon jumping out of the water. Instead, see very few. I imagine them swimming slowly and intently beneath the visible surface. The fall salmon run is a fraction of what it was 10 or 20 years ago. While watching salmon swim and span, others standing nearby told me of years when so many salmon lined the weir at the Nimbus Dam, they formed a solid bridge across the river.

Egret standing across the river in photo at right keeps a long distance from seagulls.

Mornings on Fair Oaks Bridge

Later in the morning, a dozen ducks swim in from about 100 yards away upriver. A few walkers pass and one cyclist. I hear one splash down at the river. I walk to the shallow area where salmon spawn and see 30 seagulls floating in the river looking for salmon to nibble on. Canada Geese fly in here to check status on a variety of food sources. I wonder why the Egret and the Great Blue Heron always arrive alone and stand apart from other wildlife. Sometimes I see seagulls fly overhead while driving city streets. I wonder if they are headed to the American River looking for salmon.

Do seagulls carry maps in their head? Is their navigation system similar to how salmon use their powerful sense of smell to find their home river from hundreds of miles away? This seasonal migratory habit leads them to find salmon year after year.

When a dozen ducks finally arrive they "own" the river, swimming down its center, leaving a wake behind them. Sun has finally risen over the cloud cover with a brightness that hurts my eyes. Today I hear a new bird call in addition to others I hear regularly every morning. This one is a shrill whistle – *Whoo – oo—oo. We ee oo.*

WRAPPED IN FOG

—

SATURDAY, NOVEMBER 11, 2017, 6:45 AM, 49 DEGREES

THE AMERICAN RIVER IS BARELY VISIBLE standing on Fair Oaks Bridge. Riverbanks on both the east and west sides have disappeared. Dew attached to spider webs sparkles like jewels. Sounds are muffled in thick fog. The bridge drips with moisture. A runner emerges through the fog as he crosses the bridge.

Morning dew illuminates the details of each spider webs. Why are there are always more spider webs on the east side of the bridge then the west? Is it the sun's position in the sky, wind direction, or do spiders favor the east side for another reason? I photograph several webs – drops of dew clinging to the strands illuminate these miracles of workmanship.

One pearl white seagull flies gracefully over the bridge. More gulls call out and cross an invisible river. One hour later, the intensity of the fog has decreased by least half. A heavy mist continues to bathe the river and landscape until after noon.

Mornings on Fair Oaks Bridge

RAIN SOFTENS THE LANDSCAPE

———

WEDNESDAY, NOVEMBER 15, 2017, 7 AM, 56 DEGREES

WHEN I FIRST ARRIVE, THE RAIN FEELS MORE LIKE A DRIZZLE – drops sprinkle here and there in a random pattern. The cool air and rain are a refreshing morning wake up. Even in rain, this bridge is a peaceful place to escape and watch the river move slowly downstream. Ripples and shallow places in the river change as raindrops fall more evenly and increase in number. A few people pass by. Raindrops mark the bridge deck with huge spots. Water drips down in tiny streams from the truss frame and side rails. Some people think rain makes for a dark and gloomy day. I see landscapes that are fresh, crisp, clean and bright.

Soft, consistent drumming is the heartbeat of rain. The sound of rain is a gentle lullaby. Mist softens the edges of landscapes and trees, creating blurred edges on reflected images in the water.

On this particular morning, the river belongs to resident waterfowl. I am a guest who finds joy when I overhear their squabbles, calls and comments.

Sitting at the river listening to gentle rain is its own experience. *What is the song of the rain? What is the scent it carries? Are the drops big or small? Cool or warm?*

I watch golden leaves fall gently into the river and see many others lining the bridge deck. The drumming of the rain is far louder than the soft sound of leaves settling on the bridge.

An Egret scavenges the riverbank. Finding nothing of interest, it flies away. A seagull flies in and I stand to watch its snowy white wings fly gracefully over the bridge. Ducks swim in the river, flap wildly to rise and fly away. They leave a wake behind them, accentuated by patterns of raindrops falling into the river. Rain increases and ducks ignore the event as if there was no rain at all. More seagulls arrive. They fly upstream through the center of the river corridor.

Puddles form in low spots of the bridge deck. Ribbons of water flow downstream created by the rain.

THANKSGIVING OUTDOORS

———

THURSDAY, NOVEMBER 23, 2017, 9 AM, 57 DEGREES

PEOPLE OF ALL AGES ENJOY A MORNING OUTDOORS ON FAIR OAKS BRIDGE. Families are out walking, joggers shake the bridge as they pass and I hear cyclists on the American River Parkway less than 100 yards away. The warm air is still, yet filled with the calls of birds hidden in trees that hug the riverbanks. With heavy cloud cover, the sun barely shines through. People climb the Fair Oaks Bluff to enjoy panoramic views, cross the bridge, stop a while to enjoy the river and see the wildlife at play and work.

Seagulls call as they fly over the river, some landing in the water to call again. One bird song reminds me of a calliope with its high-pitched whoop. Buffleheads skirt the water, leaving ripples as they rise and fly low across the river. Watching the river all year long, I see these daring little ducks in fall and early winter. I wonder where they live during other parts of the year.

Do birds know the difference between weekdays, weekends, and holidays because of the shifting numbers of people who come to the river? Today looks like one more workday for them in their ongoing search to find breakfast. A woman arrives on the boat launch ramp to throw seeds. Nearly 20 birds and waterfowl rush in. Seagulls call out to each other. One gull lands in the water to nibble at a dead salmon floating slowly downriver.

Photo shows reflections of clouds in the American River.

Mornings on Fair Oaks Bridge

THE WONDER OF CLOUDS

———

THANKSGIVING DAY, NOVEMBER 23, 2017, 9 AM, 57 DEGREES

GAZING INTO THE SKY THIS MORNING standing on the bridge, I wonder about the clouds - their constant motion and rich blends of color.

> *Clouds are nature's artist palette - a full spectrum of light always changing, blending and creating beautiful pictures that paint the sky.*

How exactly do they move and change shape? Are clouds held in the sky by currents of air in the same way an airplane flies? What is the air temperature inside a cloud? I have often heard, *Cloudy skies today, so our air temperature is low.* Or, *The clouds held in the heat overnight to keep away the frost.* Are clouds one of nature's mysteries? I stand in awe at how the shape and density of clouds reflect the brilliant colored lights and shadows of sunrise. Golden glows of deep orange, and varying shades of pinks, blues and grays filter the bright sunlight.

I imagine clouds to resemble unraveled skeins of yarn, finely woven baskets, and rounded puffs reminding me of spun cotton candy. Each cloud formation changes by the minute. Every new day brings a new sky landscape. With some imagination, we can find animals, dragons, giants and complete scenes roaming the skies.

Do we know if clouds move with the earth, stay in one place, or move and change shape at the mercy of winds? Yesterday morning the ground was covered in mist. The sun never shined through the clouds until evening. Sunset was a single strip of pink lasting five minutes and then faded into gray. Besides learning different names for clouds – *cumulus, nimbus, stratus* – to describe a cloud's shape, moisture content and elevation, what else can we learn about clouds?

Mornings on Fair Oaks Bridge

Mornings on Fair Oaks Bridge

DENSE FOG!

———

THURSDAY, NOVEMBER 30, 2017, 7:20 AM, 39 DEGREES

Dense morning fog creates a mystic scene on the American River at Fair Oaks Bluff. Fog hugs the riverbanks and hides the boat launch ramp.

WALKING TO THE BOAT RAMP, THE SUN IS JUST NOW EMERGING ON THE HORIZON - a golden ball in the sky. Fog surrounds the trees of the American River Parkway, as a soft white light fills the background. A circle of light shines down through the trees as if it were a spotlight on stage. Long, thin trees stand erect in dense fog. I continue walking and see the bridge surrounded by dense fog and reflecting its shadows on the water. My hands are chilled, feeling the cool, moist air against my skin. A few ducks swim to the boat ramp. One seagull swims alone. Even in the fog, these birds engage in their morning rituals – seeking crumbs, seeds, bugs or worms for breakfast. Waterfowl swim quietly through the fog as if it was not there.

A distant quack breaks the silence, followed by the shrill call of birds. A Mallard arrives with a noisy series of quacks. It swims and dives, swims and dives again, speaking of the experience between dunks. A seagull lets out a desperate call for anyone to hear.

DECEMBER 2017

———

The salmon run is ending soon. Dead salmon and a skull are seen on the boat ramp. Seagulls search for breakfast, when most of their families have flown away. They call, *Where are you? Where is the food?* Fog surrounds Fair Oaks Bridge while ice coats the slippery deck.

WHERE IS BREAKFAST?

———

FRIDAY, DECEMBER 1, 2017, 7 AM, 39 DEGREES

AS WE MOVE CLOSER TO WINTER, morning temperatures are low enough each day to bring a heavy layer of fog. I enjoy watching the mist from Fair Oaks Bridge as it rolls across the American River.

Gull in photo pauses to consider, Where do I search
for breakfast today?

The boat ramp and riverbanks are clear as morning fog bathes other sites on the American River. A single seagull circles the bridge and flies west. Few seagulls remain here on patrol as the salmon run winds down. I miss the morning calls of seagulls and the joy of watching them circle slowly and gracefully over the river.

My fingers are chilled as I stand in a frigid breeze. I wear gloves and a heavy jacket to stay warm on this cold morning. Ripples in the river trace where ducks swim through the center of the river. Low lying fog rolls slowly along the river, moving underneath Fair Oaks Bridge. Fog continues to roll under the bridge as if it was billows of steam rising and falling in a huge simmering pot.

I remember the words of a fisherman I met on the boat ramp in the fall as he was bringing his boat in from the water and attaching it to his trailer. *The best things in life you do slowly.* His words come back to me during the past few weeks since I can think of few very things I enjoy doing in fast motion. Pausing to observe morning wildlife rituals, their focused efforts to search for a meal, seeing how they relate to their own kind and other wildlife, and the waiting game to catch a single fish requires time and patience.

Muscovy duck is uncommon at Fair Oaks Bridge – a native to Mexico, Central and South America.

I am amazed to see waterfowl emerge from their overnight hiding places to swim in the river, even in the coolest, wettest weather. They talk less in colder temperatures. Today, as every morning, I hear a soft quack of at least one duck, swimming out from an unseen distance. One swims alone, dunking for breakfast. Fair Oaks Bridge rumbles as a dozen cyclists race across the bridge on their way to the Village.

Two walkers stroll by and ask, *How is your journaling going?* We often meet on the bridge. Depending on the day, I see the same walkers and cyclists. At the boat ramp, resident waterfowl come to greet me – especially if they think I carry a quick snack.

The Egret stands in its usual place on the north side of the river away from all other wildlife, to enjoy morning breakfast without company or interruption. When the Great Blue Heron arrives, the Egret flies away to escape. As the sun rises well above the horizon, the magic of morning at Fair Oaks Bridge lingers for a few more precious moments.

WHO LEFT THE SKULL ON THE BOAT RAMP?

THURSDAY, DECEMBER 7, 2017, 2 PM

I SIT ALONE ON THE BOAT LAUNCH RAMP WITH THE SEAGULL, the Canada Geese and ducks paddling around the river on this sparkling, clear and cloudless blue sky. One very unhappy seagull calls out over and over again while standing at the end of the boat launch ramp. Fifteen ducks swim and fly in shortly after I appear on the boat ramp thinking I have food. Several ducks quickly reject mandarin orange segments I bring for them. Pigeons and seagulls arrive and eagerly await their handouts.

While the ducks are busy scavenging the boat ramp, one seagull bends its head backward and screams in frustration. I imagine it is still asking, "Where is everyone? Where is the food? Why am I alone out here?"

Pigeons fly off the ramp and circle overhead three separate times before returning to the boat ramp to settle down. Ducks waddle down the ramp, returning to the river. Seagulls soar through the air with extended wings to catch air currents. The lonely gull stands on the ramp, contemplating and calls out again. Two Canada Geese arrive to wander the boat ramp looking for food.

Many dead and discarded salmon float in the river or are left on the riverbank. What creature feasted on this salmon and how did it get here?

MEMORIAL BENCH – A PLACE FOR QUIET REFLECTION

SUNDAY, DECEMBER 10, 2017, 8:20 AM, 37 DEGREES

MEMORIAL BENCH FACING FAIR OAKS BLUFF provides a place to sit and enjoy the view. This newly installed memorial bench at top of the boat launch ramp is one of many benches found along the American River Parkway bike trail to celebrate the lives of treasured friends or family members.

I wonder who was this person and what was their relationship to this place?

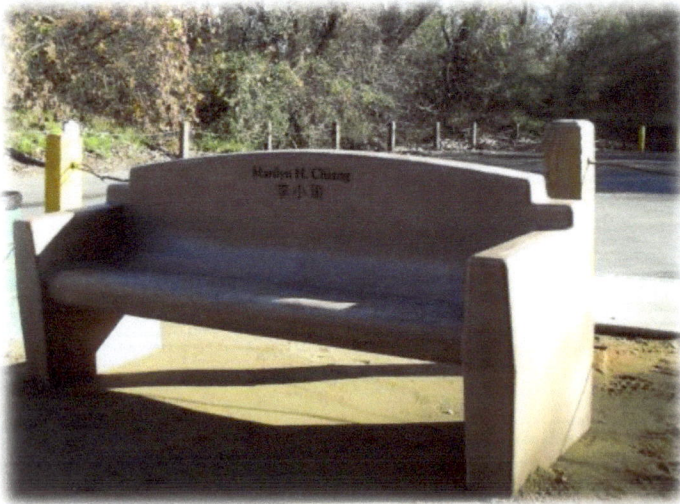

Walking farther east on the American River Parkway to the wide and shallow place, I watch salmon as they swim upstream through the current. They rise above the water just long enough to see the gray and white colors of their badly deteriorated bodies. Within ten minutes I see five salmon swishing and splashing through the shallow waters.

Several salmon circle near the surface of the water. Only their fins and top edge of their bodies are visible. Salmon splash and stir up whirlpools in three separate places. Not a single seagull is waiting here to grab a meal. Some late arriving salmon will stop here to spawn.

Turkey vultures wait in trees for their chance to feed on salmon. One searches a small nearby island for remains of a dead salmon. Another vulture was on the scene first. Guarding his salmon, the turkey vulture chases the intruder away from its catch. With flapping wings and a snap of its head, the competing vulture withdraws and leaves to find food elsewhere.

Returning to the boat ramp, I see a cyclist has arrived with a bag filled with food for the ducks. The ducks pounce on it and a feeding frenzy begins. I watch two ducks struggle to catch as much as possible. The lone seagull stands at the end of the boat ramp feeling left out. When most of the food is eaten, ducks quack all their way down the boat ramp and swim away. Pigeons are the clean up crew, snatching any tiny leftover bites.

WALKING FOR FOOD

———

MONDAY, DECEMBER 18, 2017, 8:40 AM, 42 DEGREES

I HEAR THE BIRD SINGING A CALLIOPE TUNE, WHILE OTHERS CHIRP AND HICCUP. Winter mornings are quiet here. Seagulls stand on the boat launch ramp and call out to others that can hear. I watch several seagulls fly a few feet over my head as they cross the bridge in wide, sweeping circles. Hearing their calls, I wonder are they asking, *When will it be time to leave the river?* Or, *Is there any food left to eat here?*

The parking lot behind the boat launch ramp that is usually filled with pickup trucks and other vehicles to tow fishing boats is near empty. The sound of a distant quack carries in the gentle breeze. Resident Mallards pair up and bob their heads in unison. This signals their interest in mating.

I see an Egret fly in and land on the riverbank at the foot of Fair Oaks Bluff. Goldeneyes come here during fall and winter. Egret sightings are rare. Their search for food takes them away from this part of the river.

Pigeons walk the deck of Fair Oaks Bridge searching for crumbs, seeds or remains of a sandwich, cookies and other food left behind.

FIRE IN THE SKY

FRIDAY, DECEMBER 22, 2017, 6:45 AM, 37 DEGREES

I ARRIVE AT DAWN TO CATCH THE SUNRISE, dressing snugly in my hooded jacket, long pants, long socks and gloves. Today's icy wind is just enough to keep frost off car windows and grass. Frost coats the bridge deck and I feel its slippery surface beneath my feet. My visit is short. One duck braves the cold for an early swim back and forth across the river. This densely cloudy sunrise looks as if the sky is on fire, yet the air is cold enough to coat the bridge deck with slippery ice.

MORNING CONVERSATIONS

Thursday, December 28, 2017, 8:20 am, 39 degrees

WINTER QUIET HAS SETTLED ON THE RIVER. Calm waters. No fishing allowed. River is too cold for rafting or swimming. The wildlife enjoy this serene setting with few interruptions all day long.

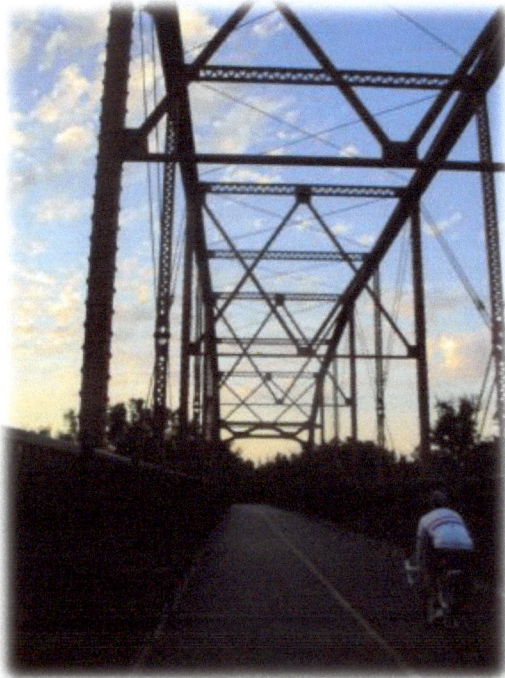

Regardless of season, Fair Oaks Bridge attracts walkers, cyclists and visitors to enjoy the scenic views by foot and by car all day long. On colder mornings, people arrive later in the day.

One morning I shared experiences with a woman who has lived on the Fair Oaks Bluff for decades. We talked what we love about the bridge, the spectacular views, the community, gardening and wildlife. She greets two friends out for a jog and we talk about the uniqueness of Fair Oaks Village.

The sky gives no hint of either the glowing orange ribbons that painted the sky or the dense fog that rolled across the across the river an hour ago. Morning air is still cold enough to see my breath.

Two Goldeneyes diving for breakfast are the only wildlife out so far this morning. Pigeons settle on the bridge truss for their morning rest. I watch several seagull pairs fly over the bridge at a very high elevation, preparing for their next migratory journey. Other pairs circle the bridge with wide, sweeping elegance before settling down into the water or to wander the boat launch ramp for a quick snack.

LINGERING FOG AND FROSTY MORNINGS

—

SATURDAY, DECEMBER 30, 2017, 7:15 AM, 36 DEGREES

SO COLD THIS MORNING, VILLAGE CHICKENS ARE STILL SLEEPING. I hear no calls good morning walking past the park and the trees that provide nighttime shelters for many Village chickens. Three chickens scratch and complain as they search for breakfast in shrubs a few yards from the bridge. The bridge deck is covered with white, slippery frost. Clouds above me resemble spun sugar in shades of gray and soft white. As the wind blows, clouds stretch into thin wisps of white. Fog washes over the eastern section of the American River. I watch as mist rolls down the river corridor and under the bridge. On this chilly morning, mist is still sitting on the river after 9 am.

The most impressive days of winter at Fair Oaks Bridge are the peaceful mornings listening to seagulls call and seeing them soar gracefully through the sky, following fiery orange sunrises, and watching fog as it blankets the river and reflects golden sunlight through nearby trees.

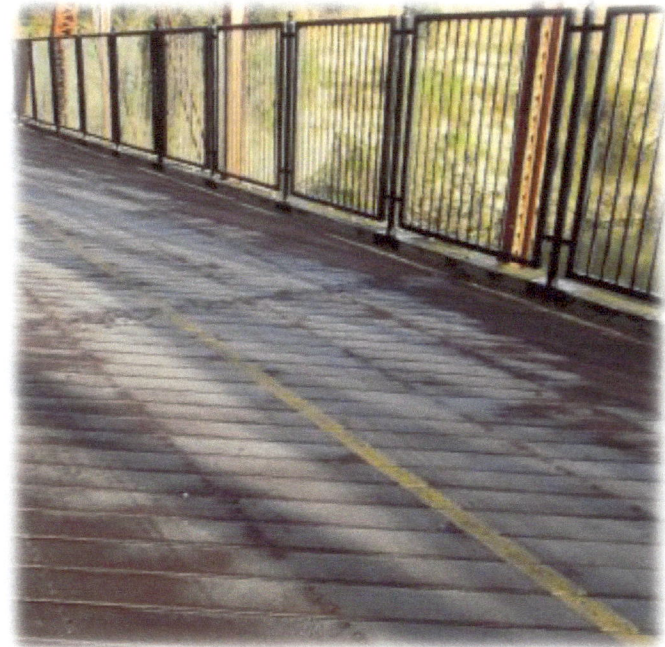

Mornings on Fair Oaks Bridge

Dense fog hovers on the eastern section of the American River at Fair Oaks Bluff and rolls slowly west. This setting reminds me of the movie "Brigadoon" – that magical, mysterious place that emerges out of fog once every few years.

Each day brings new cloud formations, and each day a new way the wind blows them apart to create a kaleidoscope of color at dawn to announce the new day. I stand watching in amazement at the fog wraps the Fair Oaks Bluff, and the sun's yellow light shines through the trees along the American River Parkway.

When I walk to the boat launch ramp, I see how the fog surrounds the Fair Oaks Bridge and drifts slowly west beneath the deck. I think of Peter Pan's *Never, Never Land* where fairies and other magic are commonplace.

Two ducks swim in the center of the river. All others are still in hiding and come out much later when the temperature warms to 45 instead of 36 degrees. Many walkers are out dressed in warm clothes and enjoying the morning. A speeding cyclist passes by pedaling as quickly as possible. An Egret flies through fog on the American River and lands in its favored spot on the riverbank at the foot of Fair Oaks Bluff. Soon two fly together and move on further downriver. I always marvel at the Egret's graceful flight, long outstretched wings and sleek, straight body.

SHARING A SALMON

SATURDAY, DECEMBER 30, 2017, 8:30 AM, 45 DEGREES

I WALK TO THE BOAT LAUNCH RAMP TO CHECK FOR MORNING WILDLIFE ACTIVITY. I find a partially eaten salmon lying at the end of the ramp. *How did it get here? How long has it been here? Why did everyone wait until I arrived to eat it?* With plenty of meat left, the salmon captures the attention of both seagulls and ducks. They take turns tearing at the salmon. Their strategies to tear it apart range from gentle poking to serious ripping. In the end, they all get something to eat – except one seagull. The ducks eat first. When ducks are done eating, one seagull drags the salmon into the river while the other wails and complains. The Pekin Duck, Mallard (on left) and Muscovy (on right) all take turns eating the decaying salmon. Pekin is domesticated and likely an unwanted pet released at the river.

JANUARY 2018

———

A small female Mallard is complaining without end – or maybe giving directions? Her tiny voice carries more than 100 yards either way, up or down the river. For several weeks, I see her near the boat ramp and hear her voice greeting each morning with *Quack, Quack, Quack, Quack.* She carries on without taking a breath for 10 minutes and often even longer.

MORNING PANDEMONIUM

———

SUNDAY, JANUARY 14, 2018, 7:40 AM, 47 DEGREES

AS I APPROACH FAIR OAKS BRIDGE THIS MORNING, THE ONLY SOUNDS I HEAR ARE MY OWN FOOTSTEPS, a few random chicken greetings and songs from birds still hidden from view. Given the degree of mist hanging in the air and the chilly temperatures, I expect to see fog covering all views on the bridge. High clouds and distant fog hung over the hills. The American River was clear without any of the characteristic mist rolling downstream I have seen on other mornings.

Two men launch a fishing boat. I hear four Canada Geese honking as they approach from the east. They are invisible until they are within 20 yards of the bridge. Then they fly over so fast there is no time to capture them in a photo. All four land softly in the river on the west side of the bridge at precisely the same moment and glide downstream. Loud honking continues as others arrive to join the chorus. Their sounds carry half mile in the still air.

On the east side of the bridge, near the boat launch ramp, one duck begins to complain. *Quack! Quack! Quack!* The chatter goes on and on without end. I am surrounded by sounds of wildlife as I stand on the bridge. Canada Geese are honking on the west side and ducks are quacking at the boat launch ramp on the east side. *It is morning pandemonium!*

I notice two dead salmon lay still in the river. No birds approach to eat them. I walk to the boat launch ramp intent on seeing the very agitated duck. Forty runners training for a marathon cross in front of me on the American River bike trail. Several cyclists followed behind the runners.

Two male Mallards and two females swim in the river near the boat ramp. One female is very upset and starts quacking again. Two minutes later, she has not taken a breath. She continues. As she swims, I am close enough to watch her beak open and close, open and close. The males swimming nearby pay no attention.

What could have upset her to inspire such a one-sided conversation?

She continues her casual swim and squawks for another 10 minutes without stopping for more than a few seconds. I still hear the distant call of Canada Geese. As the four Mallards swim away, a Bufflehead swims to the center of the river, diving for breakfast. Staying underwater for a half minute before surfacing – and then doing it again.

A ROUSING MORNING SYMPHONY

THURSDAY, JANUARY 18, 2018, 7:05 AM, 49 DEGREES

THIS MORNING I STAND BENEATH A SINGING TREE listening to another rousing symphony led and conducted by resident chickens – all still hiding for the night. I see a chicken standing in the shadow of darkness, tangled in tree branches, adding its voice to the chorus.

Heavy fog this morning and biting cold. Two Canada Geese zoom in from the east over Fair Oaks Bridge, loudly honking and honking. I hear them coming and they suddenly appear out of the fog. I catch a quick photo as they fly over before landing with a splash into the river. Two more Canada Geese zoom in from the east honking loudly, as if they are engaged in an intense conversation. I wish I understood "goose speak." Maybe they are discussing directions or where to land. They make a quick U-turn, fly under the bridge and land with a splash near the boat launch ramp.

Ducks hide in shadows of reeds near the shore. The sun hides behind a thick curtain of fog. A Bufflehead appears in the middle of the river, dunking and reappearing as it searches for breakfast in the deepest part of the American River. Four Canada Geese swim quietly. As runners, cyclists and walkers pass by I hear a "tap, tap, tap" on the bridge and then it stops. Looking at the riverbank, I notice many trees bent over so far, they brush the surface of the water. Yet their roots are still attached to ground.

I wonder where are the turtles? Haven't seen any in months. Seeing beaver and otter are rare. The Mallards are always here. No spider webs today. No spiders anywhere.

Today I brought food to feed ducks and they rush over anxious to eat. The Muscovy duck stands alone. All waterfowl keep a 10-foot distance from me. When I move quickly or walk closer to them, everyone flaps their wings in unison, flies up and heads down the boat ramp to the safety of the river. More Canada Geese fly overhead. A lonely seagull flies in squealing. After a soft landing, the gull looks around. *Am I too late? Where is the food?*

As I begin walking up the ramp to the parking lot, I hear the distinctive chortle of a Great Blue Heron as it flies along the opposite shore and then disappears into the fog. Even on clear day, the Heron is difficult to follow because its blue gray colors blend seamlessly into the hillside. I look across the river and see the Egret perched alone on a rock patrolling for its own snacks.

COTTON CANDY COLORED FOG

———

SUNDAY, JANUARY 21, 2017, 7:10 AM, 36 DEGREES

THIS MORNING'S CHILL IS NOT THE DAY FOR BEING CURIOUS, even though I can find so many things to imagine and wonder about at the river. It's freezing out here. Two chickens are awake in Fair Oaks Village calling *Good Morning* to anyone who will listen. Clouds reflecting the pinks of sunrise scatter across the sky as the sun slowly rises in the east. Today thick fog on the American River is suspended in midair on both sides of the bridge, reminding me of thin strands of pink cotton candy. I watch from Fair Oaks Bridge as heavy mist gradually moves along the surface of the river under the bridge to its western side.

The bridge deck is solid white with frost and slippery. My shoes leave footprints on the deck. Several people dressed in jackets, gloves and hats brave the cold to walk, run and cycle. Two Canada Geese fly over in silence. One Bufflehead swims in the frigid water searching for breakfast - always preferring the deepest section in the center of the river. It dives underwater and floats back up like a buoy several times over and over. A seagull preens its feathers on a tree branch leaning so far over it almost touches the water. The same branch where turtles sunbathe on warm afternoons.

As the sun rises, clouds scatter even farther apart, revealing a pale blue sky beneath. The sun peeks over the horizon and casts a bright light on the bridge. Ice crystals on the side rails and deck sparkle like diamonds when reflecting sunlight.

Mornings on Fair Oaks Bridge

MORNING COLORS

———

SATURDAY, JANUARY 27, 2018, 6:55 AM, 44 DEGREES

I CONTINUE TO BE AMAZED AT EACH DAY'S SUNRISE. A diverse palette of dazzling colors continue for 45 minutes as the spectacle of light spreads through layers of scattered clouds. On dense gray cloudy days, the brilliant colors of sunrise hide away within minutes. The most glorious sunrises last an hour or more from the first hint of light through the changing colors of clouds until the sun appears as an orange glow on the horizon.

Clouds held shades of pink from the early morning sunrise and reflected them like a mirror in the stillness of the American River.

Today the air is still with no breeze and smells damp. This is not the fresh, clean smell after a refreshing rain. This air smells like damp and stale carpet. What causes that smell? I hear the sound of a foghorn (once again) and wonder where is it coming from? I look and listen for morning patterns of wildlife during my brief and chilly visit. On this winter morning, no one has ventured out into the water yet. I stay long enough to feel the sun's heat warm the bridge.

Mornings on Fair Oaks Bridge

FEBRUARY 2018

———

I have visited Fair Oaks Bridge regularly for more than a year, through all its seasons and have come to know the rhythms of its wildlife. I ask a series of questions that still puzzle me. Even after visiting this site more than 100 times, I continue to cherish its beauty and the experience of watching wildlife wake up rituals during early morning hours.

I WONDER WHY?

—

THIS MORNING I SIT AND WONDER WHY?

I have watched wildlife morning wake up rituals, morning cloud formations and brilliantly colored sunrises for nearly 18 months at Fair Oaks Bridge. This morning I sit with questions and no answers. As soon as I think of one question, that leads me to wonder about something else. I present no right answers or facts for any question.

Why do Buffleheads dive for food in the center of the river corridor when other ducks feed near the riverbank in shallow water? Is the deep center the best place to find breakfast? How deep do they dive? What treats do they find? Buffleheads swim calmly up and down the center of the river, diving in one spot and reappearing a dozen feet or more away.

Mornings on Fair Oaks Bridge

I always look for Egrets and admire their beauty and elegant flights. I wonder how many miles they travel and what stops they make in a day? Where do they sleep? Why do they stand far away from ducks, seagulls and especially the Great Blue Heron? I see a pair of Egrets fly over and wonder why they always fly low and close to the water?

When Canada Geese honk as they fly, are they giving directions as they speak? I know the honking unifies the flock and actually helps them fly faster and farther.

I wonder where is the rain? Last year at this time, our rivers were raging torrents. I stood on Fair Oaks Bridge a year ago today and watched the water underneath it swirl and churn. I was dizzy watching. The riverbanks, the boat ramp, the parking lot and the bike trail even further back, were all submerged under several feet of water. Crowds of people lined Fair Oaks Bridge to take pictures of the wild river.

Who has returned to see the river at peace? Was the real atraction just the drama of a raging river? Visiting for the drama overlooks the larger story of understanding wildlife activity and interactions, and need to preserve their habitat throughout the year.

SPIDER WEBS – GEOMETRY IN MOTION

FRIDAY, FEBRUARY 9, 2018, 8 AM, 46 DEGREES

WARM DAY, SUN HIGH, BIRDS TWITTER IN NEARBY TREES. The Egret takes it usual place on the riverbank. The pigeons and the ducks are absent. As I walk to the boat launch ramp, a hiker atop the Fair Oaks Bluff calls to me, *Hey. There is a seal in the river!* From a distance, I can see its head just above the water. Then it dives deep and rises out of the water just enough I can barely see its head. Where did the seal come from? What wrong turn led it so far from the coast?

This morning I see a busy spider and a series of spider webs attached to the side rails of the bridge. I marvel at their precision and the geometric shapes formed in each one. Fair Oaks Bridge is a popular colony for spiders. Four to six webs are usually attached to the side rails and truss frame until rainfall washes them away.

I wonder if spiders are born with internal maps? What gives them such precise weaving skills? Which one is the lead string? How do they measure the length of each strand and intersecting line so all lines are the same length? Do spiders view their handiwork from a distance to see their progress?

THESE BEAUTIFUL DAYS

———

Sunday, February 18, 2018, 7 am, 36 degrees

MY BACKPACK, JOURNAL AND CAMERA ARE CONSTANT COMPANIONS during early morning visits to Fair Oaks Bridge, the boat launch ramp and nearby areas along the American River Parkway. Sometimes I don't have words to express the joy and delight of these experiences. The beauty of these quiet mornings is a far deeper experience than that act of writing words on a page or taking photos can express. I sit and listen. I watch and wonder.

Every morning when I approach Fair Oaks Bridge, I wonder what colors will be painted across the sky when clouds reflect the sunrise – shades of pink, fiery orange or gold? Will I see a richly colored blanket of fog rolling slowly downriver? Will clouds be reflected in the American River? What wildlife interactions will I see?

I listen every visit for the relentless quacks of the female duck as she patrols the American River. I listen for her voice far off in the distance as she swims away. I listen for the calls of seagulls and watch them soar high above me. Birds sing unseen in trees – a calliope, a whistle, and other chirps and calls I cannot describe. I often hear the chortle of the Great Blue Heron and honk of Canada Geese long before I see them.

"These beautiful days must enrich all my life. They do not exist as mere pictures. . . but they saturate themselves into every part of the body and live always."   *John Muir*

SUNRISES ON FAIR OAKS BRIDGE

I enjoy this stunning reflection at sunrise. Mist rolls over the surface of the water.

Mornings on Fair Oaks Bridge

Mornings on Fair Oaks Bridge

Mornings on Fair Oaks Bridge

Mornings on Fair Oaks Bridge

"One learns that the world, though made, is yet being made. That this is the morning of creation."

John Muir

BIBLIOGRAPHY

Dillinger, W.C. (1991). *A History of the Lower American River.* American River Natural History Association,

Carmichael, CA

Fair Oaks Historical Society, http://www.fairoakshistory.org/

Sacramento County, American River Parkway General Plan Update 2008. Sacramento County Planning Department

Save the American Association (SARA), https://www.sarariverwatch.org/history

The Face of Fair Oaks Bluff and Saving the Fair Oaks Bluff, Interpretive Panels, Bridge Street, Sacramento County

Regional Parks and American River Parkway Foundation

ABOUT THE AUTHOR

As a long time Fair Oaks resident, author and naturalist, Janice Kelley enjoys sharing mysteries of the natural world, wildlife behaviors and community stories. She provides the creative spark, provocative questions, and passion that invites individuals, youth and families to make meaningful connections with the outdoor world.

Mornings on Fair Oaks Bridge combines more than 75 blog posts first published on her website, https://naturelegacies.com. Janice is also the author of *Through the Eyes of John Muir, Practices in Environmental Stewardship*, a field studies curriculum guide; and *In Nature's Time*, book of poetry.

Janice enjoys camping, hiking and beachcombing with her grown daughter and son. They have enjoyed extended camping trips in many western national and state parks. She always packs her journal to capture the experiences in writing, drawings and photographs.

www.ingramcontent.com/pod-product-compliance
Lightning Source LLC
Chambersburg PA
CBHW041548030426

42334CB00005B/96